Zwelethu
Our land

Jaki Seroke
A memoir

TAFELBERG

Tafelberg
An imprint of NB Publishers
A division of Media24 Boeke (Pty) Ltd
40 Heerengracht, Cape Town, 8000
www.tafelberg.com
© 2021 Jaki Seroke

All rights reserved
No part of this book may be reproduced or transmitted in any form
or by any electronic or mechanical means, including photocopying
and recording, or by any other information storage or retrieval system,
without written permission from the publisher

Cover design by Wilna Combrinck
Book design by Marthie Steenkamp
Edited by Mike Nicol
Proofread by Leabiloe Molapo
Proofread by Sally Hofmeyr

Photographs inside the book from the family collection and SAP Archives
Cover photo by Tatenda Chidora

Set in Tex Gyre Pagella
First edition, first impression 2021

ISBN: 978-0-624-09190-5
Epub: 978-0-624-09191-2

Printed by **novus print**, a division of Novus Holdings

*For Mme Sinah, Mma Joe, Ntlotleng,
Lillian, Mapule, Tsholofelo, Zodwa and One,
for their glorious struggles in
the emancipation of African women*

Contents

Abbreviations	9
Foreword	11
Prologue	13
1 A Poor Mother's Son	19
2 Alex Childhood	29
3 My Elementary Teachers	35
4 Seeds of Political Awareness	45
5 Black Power	51
6 Becoming Relevant	57
7 Under the Guise of a Book Club	77
8 Devil Eyes	87
9 In Possession of Banned Literature	93
10 The Art of Activism	101
11 The Fork Ahead in the Winding Road	107
12 The Struggle Continues	115
13 The Point of No Return	121
14 Serve, Suffer and Sacrifice	131
15 The PAC Underground Expands	139
16 The Arrest in Koster	149
17 Robben Island Maximum Security Prison	165
18 Because Codesa	185
Epilogue	195

Abbreviations

ANC	African National Congress
APLA	Azanian People's Liberation Army
ASL	Alexandra Student League
AZANYU	Azanian Youth Unity
AZAPO	Azanian People's Organisation
BPC	Black People's Convention
Codesa	Convention for a Democratic South Africa
COSATU	Congress of South African Trade Unions
MK	Umkhonto we Sizwe
OAU	Organisation of African Unity
PAC	Pan Africanist Congress of Azania
SAC	Soweto Action Committee
SASO	South African Students' Organisation
SSRC	Soweto Students Representative Council

Acknowledgements

Memoirs cannot be seen as merely a solo journey of life. While the writing of this book was done extempore, the facts have been recalled with participants in the story, checked and verified to best of the author's ability. Surviving friends and comrades have unselfishly offered a hand. The author is furthermore grateful to the following:

Blacks Joyi, Mnikeli Williams, Njabulo Cele, Sylvester Ndaba, Mindlo Cebekhulu, Louis Mametse, Tshidiso Ntseki, Buhle Xaba, Marjan Boelsma, Tato Make, Ishmael Mkhabela, Lybon Mabasa, Matlhakanye Lekganyane, Malome Moalusi, Sheila Seroke, Lillian Seakgela, Mapule Shumba, Madeleine Fullard, Fred Khumalo, Kaizer Nyatsumba, and Tshepo Moloi.

Foreword

In this memoir, Seroke emulates his hero, the late Robert Mangaliso Sobukwe, who used to bend down to grab a handful of the barren soil of the prison on Robben Island, where he was locked up, and then straighten up to let it trickle through his fingers. He did that because he was forbidden from talking or even waving to his fellow prisoners as they marched past his 'house', designed specifically for his solitary confinement. They would be on their way to and from hard labour in the quarry, where they were digging out material to extend the prison around themselves.

It's poetic that Seroke titles his memoir Zwelethu. His guerrilla name in the Azanian People's Liberation Army was Zwelethu. And there are deeper layers of meaning to the title: he was born in 1960, when the slogan *Izwe lethu!* (with an open-palm salute) reverberated around the world after the Sharpeville massacre, which claimed 69 lives and left hundreds injured. The massacre occurred when the Pan Africanist Congress of Azania led a protest against the pass laws that forced every black person over the age of 16 to carry a pass at all times.

This memoir is soil trickling through Seroke's fingers: it comes in the year when South Africa and the world are struggling with the Covid-19 pandemic; it comes in the year when former president Jacob Zuma has been incarcerated for contempt of court and is facing more serious charges; and it comes at a time when the army has been ordered to help quell deep civil unrest. It comes when South Africa is at the start of its own version of the Arab Spring, when years of bottled-up anger and resentment among the masses are ready to burst out. We can hear the ominous hiss.

How did we get here? How do we find our way out? How do we correct our course? These are the uncomfortable questions that Seroke poses.

Seroke starts with the story of his birth and upbringing in the slum of Alexandra Township – grime all around him, dead dogs lying in the smelly gutters, and often dead people – victims of murderous tsotsis – discovered lying in the streets in the morning. Out of this muck, we find a growing consciousness and anger at life under apartheid.

This is a consciousness fed by family (particularly grandmother Sinah), other youngsters, teachers, and a growing number of heroes, like Tsietsi Mashinini. Seroke tells the story of his arrests, detentions without trial, torture by the security police in detention – the sarcastically named Rabasotho Police Station in Tembisa sticks out – culminating in his imprisonment on Robben Island.

In this memoir, Seroke also delineates the great irony of the liberation struggle very sharply. How did we end up here? What happened to the ideals that fuelled the struggle? What happened to the values that kept volunteers focused on the straight and narrow? Why are the names of many who made the pre-1994 vows to liberate the poor and downtrodden being called out at corruption trials and other commissions of inquiry today?

Like Sobukwe, Seroke doesn't answer these questions himself – he suggests the answers are to be sought at a fresh Convention for a Democratic South Africa (Codesa). This book is a must-read for all who love this country and care about its future.

Joe Thloloe
Writer, Editor, and Writing Coach
July 2021

Prologue

Friday, 23 March 1994. Down an eerily quiet Fox Street in Johannesburg that afternoon, two adult men engaged in deep discussions, speaking in isiZulu, sauntered ahead of me. I couldn't help eavesdropping. They were envisioning the new national parliamentary debates after the upcoming elections in April. For the first time in South Africa, the life of the black man was going to be top priority on the national agenda.

Tensions were such that a few days before, a pipe bomb had exploded near the Johannesburg Sun Hotel. The bombers were said to be right-wing extremists attempting to disrupt the elections.

'They will talk until deep into the night,' said the short fellow ahead of me. 'It will be clear who's who. Boys will be separated from men.'

'Nothing will be spared to correct the wrongs the Boers did to us. We have been under a heavy yoke for many years,' said his pal.

They turned into Eloff Street, jaywalked across the road, oblivious to their surroundings, treading softly into a future of dreams and promises that was named 'a New South Africa'.

I could see the heels and soles of their shoes as they quickly turned into Commissioner Street, disappearing like mist in the rising sun. I now stepped into His Majesty's Building where the Pan Africanist Congress of Azania had its headquarters.

Then it struck me: the new phase of our struggle for national liberation was going to be a hard slog. What with parliamentary politics and new careers for those who yearned for the limelight, things would not be easy. What with constituencies that had special needs, focused attention and high expectations, things would not be easy. I needed to back-pedal and focus on my own family, sort myself out and do what I had always passionately wanted to do: write, edit, and write some more.

The poet said, 'As others storm the Bastille, some must record the events.' The dynamics of the Azanian revolution needed to be elucidated from within, from the heat of the struggle itself. We needed to reimagine our collective past, grasp the nettle of the present, and again, collectively, imagine the future we wanted. Prose, poetry and plays were the arenas for creative writing. That was where my soul belonged, in the world of letters. I could potentially write the great Azanian novel. Why not?

Backtrack to Alexandra.

Morning assembly, April 1977, at Alexandra High School, when it was still at the Catholic church. The original school at the square and bus rank in 15th Avenue had been torched by unknown people in August 1976.

I had been 'in the struggle' against the Boers and their illegitimate regime forever. That morning I'd led a disruption of classes after we had learned that two of our classmates – Isidore Ayihlome Mbatha and Steve Tau – had been detained in the wee hours of the morning. John Vorster Square Security Branch had taken them from their homes. With a group of about forty school kids in uniform we marched in the streets singing that (John Balthazar) Vorster, then prime minister of apartheid South Africa, would never go to heaven.

Word spread fast about the impromptu march. The atmosphere was highly charged with anger and the will to respond with like for like. However, it petered out on the corner of 5th Avenue and Ruth Street, before we reached Gordon Primary School. Despondent, we went home.

If anything, I had surprised many of my peers, who took me to be a quiet and shy kid, well behaved and a model of decent behaviour.

Soon afterwards I was nominated into the leadership of the newly formed Alex Student League. It was the beginning of a life devoted to achieving national liberation. Before then I had been cautious about my participation in the struggle, more concerned with improving my social status with education. I had been to prayer meetings of the Students Christian Movement at our school. I had attended debating societies. I had even taken an interest in the South African Students Movement and their consciousness-raising gatherings. The hierarchies in students' politics were already established in these setups. Mine was just a cursory participation. The phenomenon of active participation in the struggle was an occupation for the knowledgeable and I had my own priorities, challenges, and life to lead.

You could have said my life was cast in stone. I knew that I was certainly going to acquire a degree at the University of Botswana, Lesotho and Swaziland, become a teacher or train for the priesthood, but certainly become a professional. Raise a family. Live happily ever after.

Then the student uprisings of 1976 happened. I was shaken out of my reverie. I realised that history had a mission for me. There was no turning back. Our parents suffered in silence, were cowed into sheepish submissions of exploitation and serfdom. Things had to change. We were a generation of freedom fighters spreading the gospel of Black Power. As things happened, I gravitated from the periphery to the heart of it all.

I was myself detained and tortured with electric shocks in Tembisa at Rabasotho Police Station the next year. I was later charged with possession of banned reading material. My love for literature notwithstanding, the activist in me gained the upper hand. My life was interwoven with that of the national liberation struggle.

When Medupe Writers Association was banned on 19 October 1977, I helped run the newly launched South African chapter of PEN International, an organisation of poets, playwrights, editors, essayists and novelists. I drifted into publishing and learned the ropes very fast with the Ravan Press. I was among the founders of Skotaville Publishers, then the only black-owned publishing enterprise in the literary community. My life took me to both the dizzy heights of the International Book Fair in Frankfurt, West Germany, and the dingy hell-hole of Robben Island Maximum Security Prison.

A Pan Africanist in body and soul, I was in the underground movement of the prohibited PAC, crisscrossing the country as a courier, then as an organiser, between the exiles and the home fronts. The PAC's Military Commission assigned me a more responsible role – in political leadership and diplomacy. I was imprisoned and emerged in public in later years as a delegate at the Convention for Democracy in South Africa. Barney Desai tasked me to be the PAC spokesperson.

Yet again, on 25 May 1993, I was among the more than eighty leaders of the Pan Africanist Congress of Azania arrested in one fell swoop by the Special Branch and held in detention at John Vorster Square under Section 29 of the Internal Security Act. I was picked up after a long day at the Multiparty Negotiating Forum in Kempton Park. This arrest was the last straw that broke the proverbial camel's back. The negotiations were a charade, with smoke and mirrors and sacrificial lambs.

We in the PAC leadership were the last of the freedom fighters to be hauled into detention by the outgoing regime led by FW de Klerk. Our predecessors in the PAC leadership had been kept in the dungeons 'until this side of eternity' in the aftermath of the

Sharpeville and Langa massacres in March 1960. The symbolism of prison graduates was an honour. The PAC was deeply wounded by these stratagems of the enemy's intelligence community, whose clear goals were to eliminate the organisation from ever again influencing society in the new political dispensation. The PAC was cleverly manipulated into portraying itself as a failed project in the political agenda of national liberation, and as a laughing stock when contrasted with the Nelson Mandela factor. Its resilience and survival mean that the PAC was made of sterner stuff.

My memoirs are not so much a personal history as a sociological narrative of the defiant 1976 generation. No person is an island. We are a reflection of the environment we come from. My approach is to locate the individual in their environment and mirror them as honestly as possible in their trials and tribulations of life. I am most certainly a product of the circumstances I've experienced.

We survived apartheid atrocities, I suppose, to tell the story of how we had forcibly lost our youth to the national cause in order to defeat a colossal system of national exploitation, dispossession and oppression. A critical mass of that generation became the foot soldiers and the intergenerational connection with the suppressed history of the glorious struggle. We were the rainmakers of the liberation struggle, fighting for our human dignity and the return of our land while the enemy forces regarded us as *klip gooiers* and pot-stirrers.

This book is roughly organised into three parts:
- the social background of my upbringing;
- my open defiance of the system of apartheid and settler-colonialism; and,
- the end of the repressive era, ushering in the beginnings of the new constitutional dispensation, which started in April 1994.

I came in an innocent, immersed myself in the swirl of contenders for a new society and came out bruised and broken, but with my spirit held higher in triumph. The freedom fighters won. But their ambitious leaders in the new era, betrayed by putting their long fingers into the cookie jar – the state resources – to enrich themselves at the expense of the African masses. There cannot be any more pretence of innocence or that we did not know, when the struggle enters its new phase. We must learn to move into a consolidated and galvanised preservation of the hard-won achievements of the struggle for liberation.

Mine is a story of the wretched and their fight (not their plight) for transformation and change. The fight was a collective effort, expressed from the standpoint that the oppressed and dispossessed are their own liberators.

In the Sesotho folk tale of Moshanyana Sankatana, the brave boy takes self-made weapons with him into the belly of the beast. He eggs the masses on to support the fight for freedom. Together they defeat the enemy from within. After achieving their goals, Moshanyana Sankatana is given overwhelming support to lead the people in a new environment. He tastes the nectar of freedom and the privileges associated with being in state control and leadership. The hero goes into metamorphosise and develops scales and fangs. He becomes the same image as *Khodumodumo*, the beast that was defeated.

Now, *Khodumodumo*, in its new version of Monnamoholo Sankatana, must again be defeated by the Azanian masses.

The struggle continues. Aluta continua. Venceremos, compañeros.

1

A Poor Mother's Son

Nna ke Motlase
Wa Mangako
Wa Magae
Wa Sebata
Maisa mmele go tlhajwa
Poo ya mmala wa legodimo
Seroki sa pula ya metsi
Kwena ya madiba

I have located myself in the cosmos, in the particularities of my make-up and origins. For the uninitiated, these are my praises and my clan names. The spirit of meaning in the words gets lost when translated. I am of the crocodile totem. My ancestors are of the Sotho Tswana, as academics prefer to describe us. We trace our history back to 300 AD. The research continues. We have long occupied present-day Johannesburg. Our ancestral golden city is under the present-day City of Joburg.

I was born early on the morning of Tuesday, 24 February, in the year of our Lord 1960. My arrival day on Earth was nothing to write home about. So, I conjured up these facts.

My mother responded to baby kicks by preparing herself for a check-up at the Alexandra Community Health Centre and Academic Clinic, not far from where she lived at number 155 - 5th Avenue, Alexandra.

Her waters broke when she was in a queue for the maternity section. Nurse Mary Tema, the midwife who saw to the arrival of many of my agemates, with another helper whose name I have forgotten, took her hurriedly into the maternity room and talked her through the labour pains.

She was brave, my mother. There was no epidural to ease the pain, but she did not complain. She endured the labour pains over what could have been one and half hours as she pushed me out with her stomach muscles. I, in return, headed swiftly towards the opening.

A recently qualified medical doctor from the University of the Witwatersrand, Ron Segal, attended to my arrival. He eased me in and cut the longer-than-usual umbilical cord, removing the mucus in my mouth and nose before running his fingers along my spine, holding me by the legs upsidedown with one hand, as I bawled out my presence.

Nurse Mary wrapped me in a warm, soft cloth and put me on a scale. I weighed three and a half kilograms. She entered the information on my birth registration card and then told my mother with a smile: 'It's a boy, Margaret!'

All the while I was crying my lungs out. My mother's first embrace bonded us further as she took out her breast, led her nipple to my tiny mouth, and I began to suckle. I could feel her heart pounding with joy as I sucked the milk. She made my arrival warm and most welcoming. From that moment, I knew that I was going to live and adore her all my life.

Once filled up, I slept like a newborn baby should. She also took the most fulfilling rest she had had since the beginning of the third trimester of her pregnancy.

Beaming with happiness, my mother had stipulated my names to Nurse Mary as Jaki Stone Seroke.

The story goes that her elder brother, also called Jacob Stone, had disappeared without a trace about four years prior to my arrival. Family and friends in Alex went searching for him without success. They searched among friends, relatives and acquaintances in the townships surrounding Johannesburg. They searched in the sections earmarked for black people in hospitals in Edenvale nearby and at the Johannesburg hospitals. They searched in the government mortuaries. No luck.

Some said he had eloped with a beautiful girl speaking isiNdebele. It was said that their parents had placed restrictions on such couplings, which needed to be arranged according to tribal and clan protocols. In this instance, love came, saw, and conquered.

In the Seroke family tree, four generations before me, the Bakwena people took to the story of God narrated in the Bible as brought to them by the missionaries, and they interpreted their definition of the supreme being and their gods as one and the same. Bakwena sent a delegation to the Durban harbour to meet with the arriving German Protestants, and invited them over to our lands in the present-day Rustenburg region. They converted to Christianity of their own free will. There were sceptics among them, of course. The missionaries, with excessive colonial zeal, insisted they rename everything and enforced not only a change in their image of God, but also their western Christian colonial mission.

The German Lutherans established themselves and renamed the village Madimoetsoana into Bethany. The Seroke family were among the first converts. In the cultural changes, they associated themselves with the Jacobin narrative. The biblical Jacob elected to memorialise his parents, who had blessed his imposed leadership, by erecting a stone with their names and keeping them alive in history. Jacob broke with the tradition of the elder son as the anointed leader. He also represented a departure from the traditional system of the royal bloodline. The Jacobins were republican. They were also a foundation for the rise of the national bourgeoisie. Bakwena sided with this revolution.

Each nuclear family in our circles has a Jacob who is seen as a possible head of the extended family. While it was not clear what had happened to Jacob Stone Seroke, he was clearly much liked, and my birth was seen as his reincarnation. Some continue to say he eloped over the horizon, while others believe he was probably killed in the night by tsotsis in the Dark City that is Alex.

Dark City or not, I was happy to be there.

I was born into a bondage of sorts, with legal shackles intended to make me serve as a potential labour supply to the economy, for the enrichment of a white minority that saw people of my ilk as inferior in every way. Where I grew up, we were all in a cage of oppression.

Alexandra Township lies nine kilometres north of downtown Johannesburg. It was at first a farmstead whose owner had named it after his wife, Alexandra. It became a peri-urban site for those the authorities classified as 'non-European'. The residents would be fodder for the Randlords of Johannesburg who needed labourers.

Alexandra Township had 22 avenues set horizontally and seven streets sloping down to the last avenue and the Jukskei River, which further north, joins other streams that flow into the Crocodile River in the Limpopo basin. I believe my umbilical cord was dried and sent out to the Jukskei River. I belong to the great Crocodile River. It represents my totem symbol and my spiritual residence. A crocodile must have its river. It must crawl onto the banks of the river, enjoy the mud and bask in the blazing sun. In these valleys and hills, and the scorching heat of the sun, in the mountains, beneath the bluegum trees, in the rich soil, in the rain, oh, the rain. I was born there. I will die there.

You could say that Alex was a slum. Those who owned stands allowed rooms to be erected on their properties so that they could collect monthly rentals as income. Many of the yard owners became a type of slumlord.

The authorities came to collect rent too. They used the peri-urban location laws to force property owners to have their tenants registered with the West Rand Bantu Administration Board, which was responsible for the influx control laws. The urban sprawl of Alex was methodical. The entry and exit points to the township were managed. With the madness of crowded people in the township, new unofficial paths and roads were established. These were *slangpaaie*, according to the police. Defying the laws and being unofficial was and is a way of life.

Only Selbourne Street, which cut across the middle of the township, was tarred. The rest were dusty streets. Open furrows at the sides of the streets were used as sewers at times, for the bodies of dead dogs with their distended bellies; flies and the pungent smell were dominant. Selborne Street was the spine in Alex for bus transport that ferried commuters across the township from the square and bus terminus at 15th Avenue to the city of Johannesburg.

There were no amenities except several beer halls, two football grounds, a tennis court, a theatre hall used mostly as a bioscope for feature movies, and a children's playground at the community clinic on 1st Avenue In those days and now, the graveyard is next to the Jukskei River, between Vasco da Gama and Hofmeyr streets. Night soil was collected from every yard about once a week. The yards each had a tap for running water, which served some fifteen families or more.

African families were granted freehold titles to their yards – the original stands measured between five hundred and six hundred square metres – despite the apartheid laws denying them access to land. Only a few managed to buy and own these titles. Many, such as our Seroke family, rented from the owners or the peri-urban township authorities.

The Alexandra peri-urban sprawl was a mixture of people and cultures and occupations. Everyone lived cheek by jowl: the urban wage earners and the burgeoning professional class of shopkeepers, teachers, clerks and nurses with the very poor who had left the hinterlands to eke out a living in the city. There were no tribal or ethnic separations, as tenants in the township could live anywhere they chose. There was no electricity and no street lighting at first, which was why it became known as Dark City. This let the thieves of the night have their way, and violent crime was rampant.

My parents' firstborn was Shimaboy Benjamin, in 1948. Then came Ntlotleng Rosina Elizabeth in 1953. Lucky Freddie in 1956. I was born in 1960, when my father Johannes was 32 and my mother 30. We were the baby boomer generation, coming in quick succession soon after the Second World War.

In 1960 the Pan Africanist Congress launched its Positive Action Campaign, on 21 March. They rallied the people to march to police stations to demand arrest for not carrying their passbooks. The dompas restricted our movement and stated our birthplace and work place as part of a viciously oppressive influx control system that was deeply resented.

I would have been classified as 10(1)A in my passbook because I was born and bred in the Witwatersrand urban area. Others from far-flung places would be classified as 10(1)D, for instance, to indicate their origins in a Bantustan. As far as the contemptuous authorities were concerned, we were born into subservience, working for little reward, nothing more than cheap labour.

On 8 April 1960, the PAC and the African National Congress were declared banned organisations. A state of emergency was enacted and the 90-day detention-without-trial law was implemented.

Earlier in the year, on 3 February, British Prime Minister Harold Macmillan had told the whites-only parliament in Cape Town that 'the wind of change [was] blowing through [the] continent'. I guess these were interesting times, as I began my first months on Mother Earth.

My mother could not afford all the niceties for raising a new baby. We lived with my grandmother in a rented dry-mud house. The conditions were squalid. When faced with constant poverty, a new baby to feed and care for would be seen by many as an added hardship. But my family regarded babies as gifts from heaven.

I was so sickly from poor nutrition and unsanitary conditions that many wondered whether I would survive. I contracted smallpox. They say I was a painful sight. For five days, fever gripped my tiny body. Feverish, my face covered in rashes that became blisters, and later scars, my siblings thought I was going through a near-death experience.

The nuns from the Catholic church and school in 2nd Avenue came to help. The health officials knew that the smallpox virus was contagious, an airborne disease. Babies had to be in a clean environment because they were most vulnerable. To this day, I bear a scar on my forehead from the disease.

My brother Joe Willy Karl was born in February 1963. Because of his striking resemblance to my father, he was named after him. Bra Joe was how Dark City knew our father. Little Joe was afflicted with a weeping eye as he grew up, and this affected his confidence and self-esteem. The accepted age for circumcision was two years old, but I was sick at that age, so mine was put in abeyance. The Bakwena had adopted Jewish rituals. Like the practice of bar mitzvah, we (both boys and girls) underwent a rite of passage year in the Lutheran confirmation class from the age of twelve.

When Mapule was born in December 1966, on a rainy day, I was home to see the baby girl. There was so much joy in the house. We had by then moved from the mud house to bigger and slightly more decent premises at number 34 5th Avenue. I watched the rain pounding the windowpanes as she wailed at her arrival. Mapule was the last-born child.

My maternal grandmother, Francina (known as Mme Sinah), born in 1892, was the strict matriarch of the clan. We came to know later that she was a fierce fighter. She was not meek and compliant, like women were raised to be. When the Group Areas Act further deprived African people of their pieces of ground, and her family lost their property and inheritance, she led the village protest. She bore the brunt of dispossession. Her youngest sister, Rosina Letshela (married to Levy Moalusi), was also involved in the land dispossession struggles. Their father had land taken from him by force, without any compensation. This led to a debilitating cycle of poverty. It was a bitter experience for Mme Sinah. She set up house in Fietas, an area made up of present-day Pageview and Vrededorp, near Mayfair and to the west of Joburg's business centre. From there, the family moved to Alex rather than Orlando in Soweto, which was the designated destination under the Group Areas Act. My great-uncle Jack Monageng and his family moved to Orlando East at that time.

Mme Sinah protected her children like a mother hen. They say when my father brought his friends and acquaintances to negotiate for my mother's hand in marriage, his delegation was sent packing because they were strangers and not related to the Moganetsi family – my father's family. My poor father did not know how to correct his missteps. He had broken ties with his own family, refusing to take sides in a feud. He had come to

Johannesburg looking for work. He kept getting 'organised' but never sent the proper delegation to the Moganetsi family. Bra Joe, however, had a charming smile and warm personality and would do anything to please those around him, often to the detriment of his own interests. He was a man who couldn't take any sort of pressure.

My mother worked as a laundry washer and cleaner in the northern suburbs. It was called 'kitchen work'. At the missionary schools, girls were educated up to Standard 3. They were socially designed to be extra help for white families or to be married off. My mother's parents failed due to poverty to break the buck.

My mother worked for the rich larneys of Dunkeld, Parktown and Rosebank. Poor pay was the norm. She brought us leftover food from the kitchens and cast-off clothes and hand-me-downs. She had known endurance from an early age. She worked hard, my mother.

One of our uncles, Ephraim, came to our Alex abode on a surprise visit one day. He sent me to find my siblings, and I dutifully brought them back. He then gave them all – except me – a one cent piece, the big coin with Jan van Riebeek on the one side and an Ox wagon on the other. Ephraim never came back again to visit. It was his way or no way. *Bathong!* What had I done to be denied a penny? My mother gave me her cent.

The township conditions ground us down to the point where we accepted and saw nothing wrong with living off the rejects and cast-off material from the white northern suburbs. We grew up in a world that called us piccaninnies, a world that destined us for permanent inferiority.

I believe that when I was born, a mission to change these circumstances was formed and adopted. The wind of change was already blowing.

2

Alex Childhood

Mme Sinah, my grandmother, saw to my early learning before I even attended primary school. She was such a powerful storyteller. She used words effectively, at times even roughly and sharply, to send the point home. She knew how to read a character so powerfully that, to this day, I remember some of their descriptions. She told me to man-up and be strong, whatever the outcome would be. Not to fear the consequences of standing for what was right and true.

'*O seka wa ja masepa a thaka tsa gago,*' Never fall under the shadow of your age mates. she counselled sternly. The image of eating human waste from my friends sickened me. I could not see myself ever doing that. I had to be my own man, to avoid slipping into that scenario.

She taught me to be principled and ethical. To live off the sweat of my brow. To abide by the Ten Commandments. Not to suffer fools lightly. The arc of my own character development, from my own life experience, was primarily to firm-up and survive the pebbles thrown at me by foes and friends.

'*Moremogolo go betlwa wa taola, wa motho wa ipetla,*' she counselled. I was my own liberator. Whatever medication was provided to heal a patient, ultimately the sick must themselves have the will to live and be healed.

They say Bakwena women have a particular turn of phrase and can tell with words that which is most difficult to express. I have had her words ringing in my head all my life, especially when I had to follow the dictates of my conscience.

My sister, Ntlotleng, and our cousin, Lillian, were once given money by our father, when they paid him a visit at his workplace in Killarney, and they were told not to tell anyone. No child in the Seroke household could have money without revealing its source, despite the hardships and deprivation we were faced with regularly. So, Lillian cracked easily and confessed the truth when Mme Sinah enquired. Ntlotleng refused to reveal the source of the funds.

Mme Sinah described Ntlotleng as the stingy Shylock, the Jewish merchant in William Shakespeare's *The Merchant of Venice*. My sister grew up with a crazy love of money, and we all say this about her behind her back and confirm our granny's wise words when we discuss family finances.

Mme Sinah taught me the basic skill of listening attentively when elders spoke. She introduced me to personal grooming and etiquette, and taught me how to tell the time, to set the table, and how to use a knife and fork. She detested kaffir appointments.

When she read from the Bible, the words leapt from the pages like flames in my child's mind. To use another metaphor, her words were like to the budding of a flower, the sprouting of petals. I wanted the power to do this as well. So when she found me trying to read from her books, she took it upon herself to see to my education. I believe that she made me fall in love with the written word. She called me 'the teacher'. And I would be 'the right reverend Seroke' when she was in a pious mood. I must have asked her penetrating questions. She often said, '*Nna ke modidi oo matepe*,' indicating her firm resolve to stand in her womanhood and resist all forms of enticement.

We attended the Lutheran Bapedi Church regularly on Sundays. It was a church of poor congregants in a building made of corrugated iron on 5th Avenue. Mme Sinah deliberately took us there instead of to the affluent Lutheran Evangelical Church on 3rd Avenue.

In the schism of the church, she supported the African independent breakaways instead of the mainstream missionary Lutherans. Mme Sinah was political and would often tell us how she fought against 'colour bar' policies.

She sang freedom songs to me without fear of reprisal. She taught me to sing along:

Sikhalela umhlaba wethu
Sikhalela inkululeko
Mzulu, msuthu, mxhosa, hlanganani
Sikhalela iAfrika yethu
Sikhalela ilizwe lethu!

She referred to the historical protests she'd taken part in. But none of this made any sense to me in those preschool years.

Another thing: she ran the numbers game fah-fee on the corner of 5th and John Brandt streets. This Chinese game of chance was illegal but popular because, I now surmise, the betting fee was very low. Mme Sinah taught me the numbers, and I could say them off the top of my head.

She would send me and my friends to lie in wait for the Chinaman in 4th Avenue near Fatimah's store. I would then have to drop an egg in the middle of the street as if by mistake. The Chinese man would then probably call the number representing an egg or chicken. This was a way my granny and her friends had of manipulating the fah-fee system.

On these morning forays into the dusty streets when I was sent to the nearby convenience stores (such as Tlhatlhoge's on 7th

Avenue), I had my first encounters with death and dead bodies lying in the streets. In the spooky atmosphere, there would be a mother wearing a doek, with a blanket over her shoulders, crying bitterly, as she sat beside a corpse covered in newspapers. These were outcomes of the violence in Alexandra. These close encounters with Alex ordained you a township child – pronounced *tounchip*, with ghetto pride.

The township bred mental illness. A person could explode in anger for no apparent reason. That was the psychological response to the frustrating conditions we faced. For example, an old man on 6th Avenue would talk to his small bag of tobacco, scolding it and threatening to deal harshly with the imaginary person he held by the throat. When prompted to beat up the miscreant he would slap himself hard. We children would call out *'mshaye, baba!'* whenever he walked the streets.

There was a tall boy, Madopi, on 2nd Avenue, who terrified me with his make-believe vehicle with its steering wheel fashioned from a flattened Sunbeam polish tin. It was a 'bus' and he was the driver. We always met up with him in the wrong places. He would insist that I enter the bus behind him and hold onto the belt of his short pants while he drove the imaginary vehicle. His pants were tattered and you could see his bum crack. Repeatedly he would ask, '*Uphi umamakho?*'

I soon learned to walk the streets alert to what was going on around me. Danger always lurked. It was a kind of wilderness in the streets. Once you knew how to manage the streets, you were streetwise. I had to have the street license to be regulated as a clever and not a country bumpkin. We learned in the streets; spoke its lingua franca, which our conservative parents frowned upon. Township talk gave us a sense of belonging. Of course, we also spoke all the languages that others brought to Alex. As I've said, there was no tribal affinity or ethnic chauvinism.

My brothers Lucky and Shimaboy were already streetwise. They granted me a street name, *Koko – mfana wa magrand-grand, wa marong-rong*. They were always up to some mischief. They knew what money meant, in a way that I could not understand. Once, Lucky took me to a golf course. I thought it was a game we would all play, but when I was told to carry the heavy bag of golf club, and that I was to point out where the ball had landed, I dropped everything in a fit and went home. Later, Lucky returned with money. He knew how the world worked.

Shimaboy's street name was Chingakes. His friend Tidima Ramaphakela was Doe. They picked up pieces of aluminium from the gates of factories in Wynberg and sold them off at scrap metal outlets. Shimaboy loved cars. He took me to Pretoria's Main Road on Sundays to watch rich whites leisurely drive by in their open coupés, luxurious sedans, executive combis, caravan haulers and an array of other vehicles. The fun in watching these cars that we couldn't to ride in ourselves escaped me, and I took to dodging his Sunday expeditions.

Lucky and Chingake's relationship with money ended up the wrong way. They bunked school at Gordon Higher Primary to earn themselves money at the golf course and the scrap metal shops. Each morning they would hide their school bags in the coal box and change from their school uniforms into civvies. I must have gone with my two brothers once or twice, but I could not bear to hide all day instead of going to school. So, I told my parents. My brothers often said the donkey had kicked me in the chest, and that I couldn't be trusted with the secrets of the mischievous kids. In fact they began to call me *umajika'duze*. My sister joined them. She would be out spending time with a boyfriend instead of doing her chores, and she would spin a yarn for us to tell. I would invariably disappoint her. I was always honest with my parents and I felt it an obligation to tell the elders the truth.

As far as meals were concerned, we had soft porridge and tea for breakfast almost every day. My mother was sparing with the sugar, and we children always helped ourselves to more. On good days, there was bread and jam. If there was a surprise visitor, you could have a second helping, because on those days, they always made more than was needed.

Lucky and Ntlotleng liked the crust from the previous night's pap as a snack in between the meals. Dinner was sour pap, a staple diet for the Bakwena. It would come with boiled pumpkin leaves or spinach, or, as was the norm, with fried cabbage as relish. Once in a blue moon, chicken and rice and beetroot would be prepared on a Sunday once in a blue moon.

The other families in our neighbourhood would have a different aroma wafting from their kitchens in the evenings. They had ginger and garlic added to their hot meals. They cooked bobotie. Different from our meals but equally appetising.

The van Wyks, our neighbours, did not eat offal. Their children liked us to call them to have chicken feet and intestines with us as part of what we called the 'spy diet'. Chicken offal was the main meal in our home. At Jivan General Dealer on 1st Avenue, we got curry bones and snoek. Sometimes there were ginger cakes to fill us between meals.

Lucky got a Saturday job at a greengrocer in Edenvale. He brought back vegetables that the grocer regarded as unsaleable lower-grade stuff. Spinach, carrots and cabbage were the favourites. We might not have scavenged from rubbish bins, but given the harsh township conditions, were we any different from those who did?

I reckon that the dust of the township, its darkness and lurking tsotsis at night, the gait of its women walking the streets in chemise dresses, the children playing hopscotch, the clevers against the country bumpkins, all of these things, made me. The township dust runs in my veins.

3

My Elementary Teachers

On my first day at Ekukhanyisweni Primary School, along with all the other newcomers, I was warmly received by teacher Zuma as 'her children'. She told us how we were going to make her proud. She made us laugh and sing, even if we were off-key.

Ma Zuma was a paraplegic. She used crutches and wore the boots of a polio survivor. She was a good teacher; she talked to us one by one and determined our levels, then divided us into groups A and B. I went straight into Sub B. Thanks to Mme Sinah's home-schooling, I could handle pencil and paper already, and did not need to be in the class that was still using slates.

In Standard 1 we learned to read (I found the folk tales fascinating) and write. We also learned Setswana, although the street lingo with its subculture of integrating the various indigenous languages and creating a new idiom was more dominant.

Mischievous boys in my circles were the toast of the town. Mallah van Wyk and Veli Olifant had been to Van Rhyn Stout Skool, a holding centre in Germiston for juvenile delinquents. John Brandt of 6th Avenue was a menace to all and sundry. His father sold atchar and ran a busy general dealer business. John drowned, trying to show off his nonexistent swimming skills in a stream flowing through a picnic park on Meyers Farm, towards Halfway House. Ramotlanki Modise, always up to no good in class, literally ran away by climbing out of the window during a lesson. He never came back.

The Standard 2 teacher was Ma Elizabeth Taunyane, who had a soft spot for me and my friend, Oupa Moropa. We could do no wrong in her eyes. But we knew better. We were just as mischievous as the others. Her husband was the headmaster at the local secondary school.

One day in class she came across my attempt at writing a letter and was very impressed, particularly as we had not dealt with letter writing in lessons yet. What had happened was that Mme Sinah had asked me to write a letter to my aunt in Tlhabane, Rustenburg. I showed this to the girls in my class and they took the draft to the teacher. The letter told of my brother Lucky singing 'Crying Times', a ditty by Jim Reeves. Ma Taunyane then had me sing the song in front of the class. I know I was terrible at it but she made me feel good. The draft letter became my show and tell presentation.

The Ekukhanyisweni teachers emphasised the academic side of schooling, rather than the extramural activities like choirs and sports. As a result, we were always last in the singing competitions and at football. The other six primary schools in the township taunted us and even gave us the name Mazambani – the potatoes. It was such a relief when I went to Carter Higher Primary for Standard 3. Here, our class teacher was Ma Mophosho. The naughty boys in the class called her Mraizo behind her back. She was prone to scolding us, but I thought her a good teacher and was always placed number one or two in her class. I tried to perform well in class tests. If I did badly, tears would stream freely down my cheeks. (But then, my eyes often welled up with tears when tender emotions affected me. Even when I was in a happy mood the tears rolled. I just couldn't hide them.)

The Semenya brothers, Peter and Muntu, stayed on 4th Avenue, not far from my place. We became playmates. Muntu was due for a trip to the USA, where his parents – well-known musicians – had gone to stay. Peter always had to egg him on to focus in class. Muntu irritated the teacher; his transitory status in class had taken away his ability to cope with classwork. He eventually left for America.

I recall an incident when the boys' choir teacher, Makhabishi, tried to force down my throat a blackboard duster with chalk dust, probably after I had repeatedly sounded off-key. The way he manhandled me in class made me skip choir rehearsals after that. I was stubborn like that. I liked the academic side rather than the extramural activities. I was also bad at handwork. I was not cut out for such things.

We read *Moreson Reeks Standard Drie* as an Afrikaans grammar textbook. One of the comprehension stories in it told of three unschooled urchins trespassing on a Boer's farm. They did not know Afrikaans, but one grasped *'ons drie'* and the other *'vir espress'*, while the third knew *'hoe gouer, hoe beter.'* The farmer, high up on a horse, was drawn neatly holding a sjambok. The story was about some valuables on the farm that were missing. He asked them if they knew who the thieves were: *'Ons drie'*. Why? *'Vir espress'*. Should he sjambok them? *'Hoe gouer, hoe beter.'*

There was then a set of comprehension questions to see if the class had grasped the nuances of the story. Black people were the villains. White people were virtuous.

I would often get most of the answers right. Read in context, this was blatant brainwashing of innocent kids. We were taught to obey the laws and respect the white man. I was barely eight years old when this garbage was forced down my throat.

The educational content was limited and, on the whole, boring. We boys took to playing jokes in the corners of the school premises. Sometimes practical pranks. During lunch break, we went to the corner of 4th and Hofmeyr to buy subsidised milk, cheese, and brown bread with peanut butter. It was an African Feeding Scheme project for the nourishment of local kids. We called it *abelungu* – food from the generous white people. This feeding scheme countered man-made poverty by making us objects of pity.

The boys who earned income over the weekends as caddies at golf courses in nearby suburbs were able to show off with their extra cash and would go to a fish and chips shop next to the post office in 1st Avenue, for a loaf of bread plus atchar and chips with slices of polony. These were shared among four in a *gazaat* scheme. Each had a quarter of the loaf with fillings.

My hormones began to produce a response to beautiful young girls sooner than my thoughts could process the whole game of love. I kept exchanging stares with Lerato Kgasake in class. At first, it embarrassed me that I was fixated with her, and I feared that the teacher or some of the boys would notice and laugh at me. These new feelings were strange. They brought me wet dreams and fantasies of sexual encounters I could not discuss with any level of understanding or confidence. My voice also became a thicker baritone and my Adams apple began to protrude.

I became self-conscious about my clothes. In Alex it was a shame to have no style. I did not want to be regarded as a *ngongongo*. The gents carried a yellow duster to keep the shine on their expensive shoes after walking the dusty streets. To *jewish* meant to wear stylish clothing from the shops owned by Jewish rag traders. They knew their stuff.

I wanted Lerato to love how I looked, but the child in me was playful, and I was often sweaty from ball juggling in my uniform, as all the boys did during break.

One day, a tall girl in the class, Hazel Masuku, asked me if I liked Lerato. She was within earshot and heard me say, 'I don't only like her, I love Lerato'. In English her name means to love. We laughed about that incident and it brought us together. I started carrying her school bag and walking her halfway to 8th Avenue, where she lived. Puppy love made me feel good about myself. We kissed as we parted.

Alexandra continued to be affected by the urban planning dictates and social engineering of apartheid. Families were removed to new townships, such as Meadowlands, Diepkloof and Pimville. Others were destined for townships in the east, such as Tembisa. Single male and female quarters were introduced in Alex when the Madala Hostel and the women's hostel near our place in 5th Avenue were erected.

Meanwhile I was growing up. I remember standing beneath a streetlight and sending for a girl I was getting fresh with. Promiscuity was rife in the township, and to have 'had' a girl was a rite of passage. By now I was making friends outside of the family circle. Archie and Percy Fargo went to the coloured school on 2nd Avenue. Their home was a busy shebeen and they worked constantly, cleaning and running errands. Their stepmother was an angry person who treated them harshly. I could not understand her nasty attitude towards children. They had money to spare, as they often found cash in the sofas when they cleaned. I had an agreement with them that when I went to Kings Theatre Bioscope, I would later recount for them the world of films, of imagination and the fantasies that were made in the movie world. It was a transport of joy they could not experience because of their responsibilities in the shebeen.

Their father, Norman Fargo, was a respected figure. I came to understand later that he was also a powerful gangster. He once told me and his sons that a war was coming to town very soon. There was going to be a fight for freedom. That word shook me. What was it? He said we must be ready to be freedom fighters. I had seen a film called *A Hornet's Nest* about boys living in a cage as a hiding place but providing support for the war effort and engaging in the shooting when push came to shove.

I was also collecting comics from the Jivan General Dealer. I struggled to convey to my friends the stories I read. Some of them, like Little Richie Rich, were far-fetched fantasies about the rich people of the world, a fantasy beyond my understanding. I could understand Uncle Scrooge though. There were many characters like him around in real life.

I started a football scrapbook that included my football heroes and those from the National Professional Soccer League. Displaying knowledge about the football teams and their stars gave me status among my friends. I belonged to City Wanderers Football Club. My brothers Lucky and Shimaboy were supporters of Five Special, or 5 Magidens, as it was popularly known. Everyone belonged to a team, mostly near where they grew up. I played football in the Magwaza Division and had ambitions of playing before big crowds at the local stadium.

In apartheid terms, Alex was an urban tribe that the authorities never acknowledged or recognised. It was an all-languages tribe, a conglomeration of tribes with a colloquial lingo that mixed all the native tongues. Even Afrikaans had a flytaal aspect to it, the *tsotsi taal*. Alex was a geographic area in the Witwatersrand of the time that had been occupied by a community for over more than five decades. It had a local patois, a style of living, its own camaraderie, its own disharmony and contradictions, its own sons and daughters. In jest, it was said to be the urban tribe of South Africa.

The Seroke family were removed to Tembisa near the industrial belt of the East Rand. It was an expansion of the big manufacturing concerns and small factories in Isando and Kempton Park, near Jan Smuts Airport. We were taken there to improve the supply of cheap labour to these areas. Despite this, I chose to travel by bus every day to Carter Higher Primary School in Alex. My brother Shimaboy also commuted to work at a panel beater's shop in Wynberg, on the outskirts of Alex.

The chairman of the parents and teachers, association was Rodger Sishi. He was also involved in the management of the National Professional Soccer League. The school principal was Simon Mpatlanyane Lebeloane. They addressed our class to motivate us in preparation for the IQ test that might allow some of us to skip the Standard 6 class and go to Alexandra Secondary School. The parents had a high regard for the local secondary school and were focused on the Junior Certificate class in Form 3. It was the silver standard. They all wanted their kids to wear the uniform and stepped onto its grounds. It was a measure of success in the community. I was seen as fortunate to have made it into the school.

Lebeloane encouraged us to become professionals: doctors, teachers, lawyers, or whatever else we fancied. We were going to make him proud if we went on to attain higher learning. He imagined a future where in his old age, if he were to be sick, a doctor from this class was to attend to his illness. He made us laugh, acting the sick patient, nagging the nurse and the doctor. He made his point. Education, education, and more education. (Unfortunately, he died in a car accident in Tembisa.)

My class wrote an aptitude test in 1973, and six of us, two boys and four girls, were sent to Alexandra Secondary School to start Form 1 in May of the same year. A new extra classroom was set up for us because there was no space on the school premises. The classroom was a gym facility at the main entrance of the stadium on 12th Avenue. It was overcrowded, at about 64 pupils in one class, taking lessons from one teacher, and doing the best we could under the circumstances. (Ironically, I had used the very same gym facility to learn boxing.) We had the crème de la crème of the bright pupils of Alex in the class. Every higher primary pupil in Alex contributed their best brains.

Alex Secondary was built using a community fund championed by Leepile Taunyane, who became the headmaster. Its motto was *Labora omnia vincit*, work conquers all. I regarded my schooling as the Taunyane route, with Mrs Taunyane in elementary and Mr Taunyane in secondary school. The English teacher was Leepile Taunyane. He said we had to read if we wanted a good command of the English language. He spoke a language I understood. The seniors spoke English fluently.

The teachers were a mixed bag. Some were inadequately trained and could not handle their subjects very well. Others were experienced and had university degrees.

In 1974, I took Saturday classes for confirmation as a Christian at the end of the year in the Lutheran Church, Sebo saka parish, in Tembisa. My brother Lucky had stopped schooling and was a sometime factory worker. He took to hard drinking and failed to attend the confirmation classes.

Unfortunately, my parents' low wages could not pay for my fees at school, clothing, bus fares, and other expenses, so my sister Ntlotleng kindly took care of me.

By now my social awareness was broadening as I saw the odd ways in society and read widely, beyond prescribed books, to enhance my understanding. What was clear to me was that ours was a wretched rat's life.

Street fights involving gangsters were a regular thing. Our yard had graffiti at the entrance and 'Valley of Tears' written in big letters. The boys of the area became the Valley of Tears gang. We had others such as the Top Sevens, the West Coasts, the Hazels. All interschool competitions became turf for gang warfare.

My friends and I attended boxing lessons run by Chappies Setshedi in a classroom at Ekukhanyisweni. I was thin as a rake. The gym exercises made me fit but I was not putting on any weight. Then Chappies was killed in a knife fight in the streets. This was the way life came to be: someone you knew closely dying over the weekend. The boxing club was transferred to Jersey Joe on 12th Avenue, at the stadium sports facility. In boxing, we were being prepared to stand our own in the streets or to become great fighters in the ring.

We were discouraged from joining gangs or getting involved in street fights. You could fight only to defend yourself or those who were weaker and vulnerable.

Many of our elders had belonged to the notorious Msomi gang of the 1950s. Others had belonged to the Spoilers or the Americans. They copied the gangsters they saw in the movies.

Eventually in Tembisa there was a turf fight between the Dindelas (removed from Edenvale and Germiston locations) and the Kwaito gang (from Alex). It was a senseless and stupid fight that entrenched the wretchedness of slum life. It was the wrong way of surviving the oppression.

4

Seeds of Political Awareness

My voracious reading was beginning to bear fruit. Schoolwork and the literature recommended by teachers overcame the trash I gobbled up in my general thirst for knowledge.

I had started with photo stories and upgraded to Marvel comics. The James Hardley Chase novels were on my reading list. I read everything available, including magazines such as *True Confession*. Women in my neighbourhood passed on any chick lit they'd read. My mother brought me the biography of Golda Meir, the prime minister of Israel. She might have been given this piece of propaganda by her employees in Dunkeld. Nevertheless, I read it from cover to cover.

My father was a general helper at Ster Kinekor cinemas in Killarney. He collected trash for me to read: it was trash, but as I said, I read anything.

After reading, soccer was a big thing for me. My friends and I supported Highlands Park Football Club, nicknamed the Mean Machine. Eventually the owners sold the team when the National Football League merged with the National Professional Soccer League.

I remember that there was a special place for black spectators behind the southern goal posts at Balfour Stadium. I have a memory of Baba India of Blackpool Football Club in Alex lashing his long sjambok on the field at half time, almost playing the shaman of the team. But all the time we were enjoying ourselves

I had an awareness of the apartheid laws; they were too much in your face to ignore them.

And then Toto Skosana, a fellow student at Alex Secondary, appeared in *Drum* magazine protesting outside the Magistrates' Court and being molested by the uniformed police with Alsatian dogs. He chaired the South African Students Movement meetings. At that stage we had created a debating society at Alex Secondary, chaired by Ben Mhlongo. The intention was to prepare students for public speaking, and we always managed to attract a full house.

When the workers at the Heinemann electrical factory in nearby Wynberg launched a strike for their rights, better working conditions and pay increases, the police set Alsatians on them, too. My sister Ntlotleng was an employee at the firm and told me how badly things had gone down. State harassment was everywhere, even outside the country; people such as Onkgopotse Abram Tiro were being killed by parcel bombs while in exile in Botswana. Then there was the appalling treatment of Sewsunker 'Papwa' Sewgolum, the golf champion, who was made to stand in the pouring rain to receive his award after winning the SA Open Tournament against white hopefuls like Gary Player. This riled us and we began to discuss these matters at the debating society, along with the apartheid sports policies and unjust laws such as the Group Areas Act, the Immorality Act, the Separate Amenities Act, the Bantustan laws. They were all thorns in our flesh.

Themba Sishi, who taught the English class, encouraged us to study beyond the Junior Certificate and get a matric, and possibly then a university degree. He got us reading the daily newspapers such as the *Rand Daily Mail* and *The Star* to improve our vocabulary and to keep up with important news.

The *Rand Daily Mail* had a regular Wednesday column written by South African Students' Organisation leaders expounding on the Black Consciousness philosophy. Their use of English was high-flown and not easy to understand, but their articles were always topics of discussion for us.

While politics featured heavily in our discussions, we also had to contend with the rougher side of life. On one unfortunate occasion our school hit the front page of the *Bantu World* when some of the school kids on a trip to what was then Lourenço Marques (now Maputo) in Mozambique got drunk and were photographed holding bottles of liquor. It was disgraceful. But that wasn't the only occasion. We had to witness some of the pupils being arrested at school for criminal activities. Alex was a breeding ground for tsotsis. There was a story in the *Rand Daily Mail* about hijackers who stole a car in Highlands North and drove it to Alex, where they discovered a toddler quietly sucking at a milk bottle in the back seat. At least one of the thugs had the gumption to return the car to its owners and the child's parents. Crime was commonplace but that didn't make it right.

Some teachers, such as Abel Baloyi, enforced discipline through corporal punishment. I recall another teacher, at Carter, using thick wire to lash our buttocks. Baloyi also punished latecomers by making them clean the schoolyard. At some point graffiti in the boys' toilets called him a 'barking dog'. Some likened him to Field Marshall Idi Amin of Uganda, while others said he equalled the cruelty of the notoriously brutal Brixton murder and robbery squad.

In 1975 the school hired a new headmaster – Peter Rikhotso – to replace Leepile Taunyane. Rikhotso had been detained for three years as a political prisoner on Robben Island. His crime? Persuading his pupils to participate in the activities of the banned PAC in 1963. He taught me history in my Junior Certificate year, and later English when I was in matric. His teaching experience came in handy in the turmoil of the student uprising in 1976, as he could contextualise the political issues in the country. He taught us to seek our own answers to contentious matters.

In March 1975, Mme Sinah's death marked a turning point in my understanding of society. The news of her death was conveyed to us by a nurse at Tembisa Hospital, where she had died. I was shocked. It was the first time someone so close to me had died. She was buried two weeks later. But that was not the end of it. The Lutheran church was not available, for some reason, to conduct the service, which was a shocking betrayal of her beliefs and commitments. Her life had been devoted to the church. I took this harsh response badly. It made me question the point of good behaviour, and I stopped attending Sunday services. I was not going to be dished out the same fate as my grandmother. It was then I realised that my family was dirt poor and trapped in poverty beyond the abilities of my parents to rise from it. My family members eked out a living through their menial jobs. And this poor status meant that others treated us badly. I began to realise, too, that the future looked bleak. For example, my desk mate in class, Andries Tshediso Ntseki, was more political than I was. One of his uncles had spent ten years in prison on Robben Island and had educated him about our political and social standing – or non-standing. Andries and I felt that even with university degrees, it was still going to be difficult to find suitable jobs as black people, especially as the job reservation law confined us to menial jobs.

In my class at the time was Johannes Boyce Bohale, another one who was well versed in political issues, and he had a cousin in exile with the ANC. In many ways I was fortunate to be surrounded by knowledgeable peers. So when one of the teachers organised odd jobs for us pushing trolleys at a bottle store, we refused. We were not going to be hewers of wood and drawers of water for white people.

I have to say that our teachers were also doing their best to broaden our minds. We were taken to the Johannesburg Art Gallery; I was encouraged to write for the newspapers, even letters to the editor; we were encouraged to meet painters; and we were taught the works of local poets such as Wally Serote, who had recently published his first volume of poetry, *Yakhal'inkomo*. This was also the title of a popular long-playing record by Mankunku Ngozi. These were creative people living among us, and because of that I felt that there was some hope.

In my own writing, I gravitated towards poetry. My first attempts were shameful. They sounded like John Donne and William Wordsworth. Then I came across a copy of *Sounds of a Cowhide Drum* by Oswald Mtshali. It was exciting, and because of it, I changed my writing style.

Of course there was also schoolwork to focus on. I had my Junior Certificate year to finish. My grades in Afrikaans were fair and I had no reason to complain. I had grown up in an Afrikaans-speaking community and we'd played children's games in Afrikaans. I also loved its expressive language. I thought the Afrikaner poets, such as Totius, were playful with words and very imaginative.

I also began to think about the Setswana poetry we had as classwork. One teacher started delivering tutorials in Setswana when she was a student teacher at Carter Higher Primary. Many a time she punished me with cane beatings on the palm of my hand for my poor performance. I never could work out why she unleashed her frustrations on me.

Her attitude didn't put me off languages or writing. The creative bug had bitten, and I began to read with a purpose. I wanted to be an author with books bearing my name in the bookstores and libraries.

I knew that I would have to do as my grandmother had taught me: *'Go tlosa bubi mo matlhong'*. I had to make an effort to clear my vision and see my world for what it was. And the best way to do that was to gain knowledge and be informed.

5

Black Power

June 1976. The midyear exams were finished. We were not in class. At the end of May, there had been an altercation between pupils and police at Naledi High School in Soweto, and a police van had been set on fire at the school when the cops arrived to arrest one of the pupils. This incident might have escaped the attention of most, but for me, any political developments at schools were beginning to mean a lot.

I was home in Moteong Section in Tembisa on Wednesday, 16 June 1976. Even though news broadcasts by the SABC were taken with a pinch of salt, when I heard a report of Soweto students injured and killed by the police in a street protest, it got my attention. And that of many others. It was discussed with great concern in my neighbourhood. People were angry, with the moderates blaming the unrest on unruly elements or Black Power radicals. The majority were excited by the uprising and the looting of bottle stores owned by puppets of the white man. Government buildings were torched randomly. I thought of it as Armageddon.

Television broadcasts had started in 1975, but a year later few black families had TV sets in their houses. In any case, the programming appeared to be aimed at the white folks and centred around issues that would appeal to Afrikaans-speaking audiences. On that Wednesday evening, the radio stations were abuzz with reports of two deaths in Soweto. The announcement of a white official who had died also took centre stage in the news.

The next day at Tembisa High School (one of two high schools in the township), pupils stopped classes and headed for the streets to march. Among the leaders were George Moyo and others I knew well, including Ben Mhlongo.

On Thursday, the protests and shooting by the police were reported to have spread to Alexandra. Phillip March, who attended the coloured school there, was shot and killed on 4th Avenue. In Alex and in other townships, shops were being ransacked and looted. The West Rand Bantu Administration Board premises were set on fire, and chaos ensued. This was repeated in the East Rand communities, with shouts of 'Black Power' and raised fists demanded of everyone from Natalspruit to Kwa-Thema, Duduza to Wattville.

Two weeks later, our school facility on 15th Avenue was burned to cinders.

Police searched throughout Alex for the ringleaders, and raided the family homes of many schoolchildren. We learned that one of our classmates, Boyce Bohale, had skipped the country. So too had Toto Skosana and many others.

We had no school to return to when the winter recess ended.

That year, 1976, was the year of fire, the year of ash. It sparked pent-up feelings of frustration borne of the restrictions and oppressive conditions meted out to black people, and it encouraged them to act. An axeman went to Johannesburg's central business district to chop up whites randomly in the streets. He made the news.

The main focus for us was on Tsietsi Mashinini, who belonged to the South African Students Movement and was assigned to lead the Soweto Students Representative Council. This new organisation comprised two representatives of each secondary and high school in the township of Soweto. It raised the students' grievances and interacted with the Black Consciousness organisations. The Soweto Black Parents Association was formed to liaise with the community on the issues that needed immediate attention. And there were many such issues.

The detention of schoolchildren made it difficult for school to return to normal. The SSRC attempted a march to John Vorster Square police station in central Johannesburg, where the police were known to torture and keep the Soweto kids in solitary confinement. The Black Parents Association members were themselves detained when they raised these concerns. Tom Manthata and Winnie Mandela were among those detained.

Tsietsi Mashinini was on the run. He was so badly wanted by the apartheid authorities that they placed a ransom on his head. The SSRC leadership were either being detained or were reported to have left the country, fleeing from harassment by the Special Branch. Mashinini was said to have reached the United Kingdom and was being hosted in London by big-name personalities in the arts, such as Margaret Wingrove.

A classmate in Form 1, Ernest Abrahams, who had an affinity with political developments from a young age, was reported to be in Dar es Salaam, Tanzania. Khotso Seatlholo replaced Tsietsi Mashinini as SSRC president. I knew Hans Seatlholo and his cousin Hendrick Marothodi Seatlholo, as we had all been in Ma Mophosho's class at Carter Higher Primary. They stayed at 52 6th Avenue. Their father, Kerry Seatlholo, was a shebeen owner and well known as a gang leader of the Americans in the 1950s. He was detained in July 1976 and later charged in a terrorism trial with members of the African National Congress at the Old Synagogue Magistrates' Court in Pretoria. Elsewhere, at the University of Zululand in Ongoye, students who had protested against the KwaZulu homeland authority were expelled as troublemakers and not accepted back when they reapplied.

I had knowledge of these developments because I read *The World* newspaper daily. Its editor, Percy Qoboza, wrote interesting articles about the uprisings in almost every edition. Suzette Nxumalo wrote a regular column providing a perspective on the Soweto kids roaming the streets without access to their schools. There were many other articles by black journalists about the steps taken to resolve the impasse between the security forces and the pupils. *The World* gave a voice to Soweto residents.

I collected newspaper clippings about the June 16 uprisings and took to reading all relevant information about the students' struggles. This was my way of following from the side lines. I also read my schoolbooks, because there was an assurance from the Bantu Education regional office in Johannesburg that schools would open soon, possibly without Afrikaans as a medium of instruction.

Alex High School now moved to the Catholic church premises on 2nd Avenue. The facility was no longer in use by the church and the classrooms were almost acceptable. However, there was a need to replace broken windowpanes and for proper maintenance of the premises. While we returned to school, members and leaders of the SSRC were continuously hunted down. News reports had Khotso Seatlholo surviving bullets shots at him at night by what could have been police in disguise. The conflicts with the apartheid regime were now a matter of life and death. The polarisation dug deep, with no hope in sight of a peaceful resolution.

What remained of my class of 1976 wrote the year's final examination in January 1977. I started in the next form in March of that year. As senior students in the high school we fell to discussing the state visit of Henry Kissinger, the USA's Secretary of State, and that of Nikolai Podgorny, a senior statesman from the Union of Soviet Socialist Republics (USSR), as if our lives depended on it. The teachers prodded us to raise the bar. We grappled with concepts such as capitalism, imperialism, colonialism, superpowers, Black Consciousness, Afrikaner nationalism, Pan-Africanism, and many other interesting matters in our schoolwork.

The senior classes had new pupils from other areas outside Alex. They came from as far afield as Katlehong on the East Rand or from boarding schools in the rural areas where they had stoked unrest and been sent home for not complying with disciplinary procedures. Others were faced with changed family circumstances and could no longer afford to be far from their families in Alex.

In essence, 1976 politicised the classroom and captured the imagination of young people as never before. It hit me straight in the face. It was no longer possible to live with fanciful dreams about the future when the reality of being an outcast and a possible outlaw were greater than at any time before. The innocent blood of schoolchildren shot by the police in broad daylight had run in the dusty streets, had run with the dirty water down the sewers (where there were sewers). I knew then that I would have to find my place somewhere in that generation of protestors. It was a winter of discontent, a season that would not end quickly enough. It formed a new generation of the struggle.

The 1976 uprisings challenged the system of apartheid and white domination. We knew we had to fight it to the finish, because it held no future for us.

The homelands, the new political name for the Bantustans, were being set up for every indigenous language group, and black people were being rezoned completely out of the urban areas. The effect of this system was that once each tribal group reached sufficient levels of co-operation with the Pretoria administration, they would be handed quasi-independence. Transkei was said to be the first independent state and was pronounced as such in 1976. Bophuthatswana, stretching into pockets of the western Transvaal, the northern Cape Province and the Orange Free State was also applying for independence in 1977. Connie Mulder, the Minister of Plural Relations and Development, said his charges, the natives, were temporary sojourners in South Africa. John Vorster, the prime minister, was emboldened to keep his jackboot on the neck of the people.

6

Becoming Relevant

It dawned on me one fine morning that my dreams of studying to be a teacher or qualified professional would not be as easy to achieve as I had hoped. The university campuses for black people were a battlefield, in the same way that the township streets were dangerous for schoolchildren. There were obstacles on this path in every way imaginable.

My father lost his job at the movie theatre when it was turned into a studio for the new burgeoning film industry and all surplus employees were summarily dismissed. My father had no skills in the business. He was a non-person, fit to be chucked out without a thought, like used bubble gum. Many like him were made casualties very easily. He left the way he had come in, with nothing to cover him when he was unemployed. Just like that. No safety net. He resorted to running the numbers game for the Chinese, as my grandmother had done. The attraction to gambling seemed to run in the family. It gave me the shakes to imagine myself cast into that mould.

The hardships at home hit us hard then.

I depended fully on my sister Ntlotleng for everything. She, too, earned a pittance as a factory worker. She had sacrificed her income to support my cousin Lillian, who had fallen pregnant in her teens. Baby Mike was born in February 1972. We all showered him with love and care, but he had, in reality, been born into a family that desperately needed upliftment from the cycle of poverty.

My brothers, Lucky and Shimaboy, had not turned out well, and had no idea of the suffering and degradation that we were going through as a family. Lucky drank away his meagre earnings from South African Airways, where he did odd jobs at the aircraft plant. Shimaboy could not part with his money. His money was his money. We called him Bobby Locke behind his back. No, not after the prowess of the golf champion, but because his pockets were locked. Shut.

Looking around at my neighbours, the immediate community, my friends and their families, everyone that we knew, our poverty was normal. Those who had working parents or were from stable families were few and far between. They were called tycoons. This was just a word we used without understanding its real meaning. Everyone eked out a living in my surroundings. The reality had me crestfallen and disappointed. Despair loomed large.

My only chance to rise above this was through schooling, matriculating and perhaps getting another qualification. That way I could potentially earn more and get my family out of the mire of poverty. I already had my Junior Certificate qualification. I was seventeen and had an opportunity before me to go forward.

I was dead against earning extra cash on the golf courses as a caddie. The caddies I knew were smoking pot and drinking heavily. They wore smart and expensive clothes but were not good company. They often fought among themselves in the shebeens over girls.

I liked it that our school principal had been arrested for political offences before and had spent three years on Robben Island. Although he didn't talk about it, it gave him a certain status. He taught me English and history and I valued his every word. He was sharp, and yet he seemed absent-minded. He pointed out that in English you don't say 'do favours'; you 'curry' favours. This and many other distinctions in the usage of the language often had me fascinated. He said history was not made by the people named in the history books, but by a collection of people who were the wheels of history. My mind went bonkers. He taught us that a woman was a paragon of beauty and went on to ask us to find a better way to put it than that. It blew my mind. He said schooling was meant to make us think on our own and find the answers to our problems.

Peter Rikhotso had replaced the charismatic Leepile Taunyane as headmaster in 1975. Taunyane saved us from becoming rascals in society. Rikhotso conscientised us regarding the circumstances we came from, and made us consider being objective and relevant.

I was in Class B and we were behind schedule in the school syllabus. We had started late in March and had to catch up. Class A comprised new students and was well on its way with the schedule. They had tension in the class about the role of the youth and students when the prevailing politics of protest were discussed. A coterie of articulate classmates apparently began to occupy the vacuum of student leadership. They opposed the prefect system that the school authorities were intent on initiating.

The John Vorster Square Special Branch must have had their sights on these developments in the class. Steve Tau and Isidore Mbatha were picked up in the wee hours of the morning. Two others, Sylvester Ndaba and Zebulon Mandla Cebekhulu, were raided, too, but were not at their residences. The next day, when the school assembly dispersed, the students were restless and reluctant to go to class, particularly the senior classes. My gut reaction was that we needed to take the matter to the streets immediately. The others were still doubtful or fearful about what to do. I gathered around those interested in action, agitating that we must hit the road. The girls were for action. We grouped around the entrance gates and used the grapevine to spread the message that we were going to march. When we had gathered sufficient numbers we started walking, singing freedom songs. I was in the front pumping my fist in the air and calling for Black Power.

I came to learn that political observers on the school premises, particularly teachers, started describing me as a 'relevant student'. Being relevant was a political description of a socially active black person working for the common good of the community and opposing the white power structures. It was an honourable position.

On that day, our march entered M.C. Weiler Primary School and all the children were sent home by the principal, Mme Phale. We walked on with increasing numbers towards Gordon on 5th Avenue. But then my team of girl leaders decided enough was enough. The point was made. We should call off the march. True. We had not planned where it was going. The disruption was sufficient.

Nevertheless, we were resolved not to go back to class while our student leaders were being tortured in detention at John Vorster Square. The next day there was also a call for a schools, shutdown throughout the township.

The church leaders then called a multidenominational forum chaired by the Reverend Sam Buti. They understood the issues and approached the school board, demanding the release of the two detained students. Sylvester Ndaba came to me and said that we had to liaise with leadership structures to monitor events and lead the school community in Alex.

Interestingly, Sylvester was a teen idol since he had appeared in an advert for Salusa 45 together with an English football star, Stanley Matthews. The advertisement ran regularly in the newspapers and magazines I read. I also knew Norman Ndaba, his elder brother, who had been at Carter Primary and was one of the seniors then. Sylvester's name on the streets was Lawani. He told me that it was given to him by his father's friends because he was noisy and disruptive as an active child in the house. *Lawani* is *tsotsi taal* for noise. I also knew Rev Sam Buti, who was from the Dutch Reformed church on Selbourne on 5th Avenue, from before our forced removal to Tembisa in 1973.

We held meetings of student leaders and decided on a formation unique and relevant to our Alex realities. It could not be an extension of the Soweto Student Representative Council. All the same, how we constituted ourselves was largely informed by former Soweto students such as Ndaba and Mbatha. We also had to include the likes of Thabang Makubire. He was a matriculant from Bethesda College in the eastern Cape Province, a member of the South African Students Movement, and friends with Barney Mokgatlhe and others who were close to Tsietsi Mashinini. Barney Mokgatlhe was now in exile with Tsietsi. These were persona non grata students involved in the struggle.

The system – as we code named the state apparatus to police activists – had a coterie of informants at every level. It also came to be known that the system had infiltrated every organisation of resistance to keep tabs on what was being planned and implemented, and who the 'instigators' were.

Those who interacted with the SSRC in our group were on the run from state harassment, like Thandi Mnyele, daughter of the priest at the African Methodist Episcopal church on 10th Avenue. It was the order of the day to run or be detained for an indeterminate period, where you faced the possibility of torture and even death. In 1976, the announcements of death in detention came in thick and fast.

Khotso Seatlholo had skipped the country after he was hunted down. Dan Montsisi, the next SSRC leader, and several others in the SSRC leadership were raided and arrested. They were kept in detention for what seemed like forever. Meetings with Montsisi's leadership had taken place in the Alex chapter. It would appear that this was also known in the corridors of the Special Branch.

The next SSRC leader was Gordon Trofomo Sono. We would need to liaise with the SSRC under his care to establish formal relations, although with leaders on the run, meetings were not easy to arrange.

It so happened that after a group sleepover on 7th Avenue, the family there was raided a few days later and harassed for harbouring high-school learners. We decided not to go out in groups again and spread out in ones and twos.

One of the history teachers, Sipho Zungu, organised a night out at the Market Theatre in Newtown, to watch the play *The Island* by the Serpent Players from Port Elizabeth. It was a two-hander performed by the actors Winston Ntshona and John Kani and written jointly with playwright Athol Fugard. We had an entertaining evening; the play described the experience of political prisoners dealing with the challenges of confinement, lost opportunities, character development, and a recreation of Antigone as a story within a story. We were blown away by the message of true brotherhood conveyed by Ntshona and Kani. They called each other by the Afrikaans term of endearment for friends and brothers – *broer*. After watching this exciting play, we started calling each other *broer*. Every time we met; it was a meeting of the *broers*.

I started to see the potential of the arts to mobilise the community. Poetry performed and recited on stage reached the crowds much better than elaborate speeches. With hindsight, my first attempts were funny, and not meant for anything other than expressing our anger at our oppressors. Nothing creative other than raw material without the emotive expression or deep intensity of the arts.

Poet Sipho Sepamla came to Thabisong Youth Club, invited by the social worker heading the institution, Maggie Makhudu, to interview both Hlome Mbatha and Vester Ndaba. Mbatha and Ndaba were on the run from the Special Branch and had been in solitary confinement at John Vorster Square. So, poets did not only dream up words and string beautiful verses together. They went to get the heat of the experience. I was certainly going this way. Thabang Makubire also wrote poems, throwing in idioms like *ukutsotsobala*, to be out on the run, to spice up the poetry for his audiences. We often shared our writings. We were the dreamers of freedom in the group.

When we met to formalise the student leadership structure, deciding on the name was a political exercise in itself. Thabang moved for a name that linked us with the history of African resistance to colonialism represented by the banned Pan Africanist Congress and African National Congress. This was provocative. He was supported in the meeting when he said we could not be the SRC of Alex because that could immediately put us in danger of being hunted down by the Security Branch. Of course we recognised the irony that two of our members had already been targeted by the Branch. In the end we settled for the name Alex Student League, taking the argument that the Youth League had shaken up the old guard of the African National Congress. This was what the 1976 generation was doing to the nation, after the prohibition of the PAC and the ANC, and in response to the oppression under which we lived.

In Alex, the generation of the Youth League walked anonymously in the streets, and young people had no knowledge of who they were, because the Special Branch had made their history a crime. We all agreed, we were bold to take this stance.

Even though I was known to be reticent, I excitedly expressed myself in the meeting as being against white minority rule, and

I would possibly have been with the breakaway movement from the ANC, the PAC. I was for Africanist Black Consciousness, if there was such a thing. These views marked my arrival in activism. My nickname was Zwelethu, on the strength of the PAC rallying cry and the open-palm salute. I used the palm and the fist interchangeably. One of our number, Matoto, brought recordings of the speeches of Malcolm X, and that became his name. The Afro-American struggle activist represented our own struggle. We used their idioms and manners of promoting the black experience. We were now relevant to the circumstances of the black man's reawakening, *broer*. We were a band of brothers and sisters.

Police harassment set in as we expressed ourselves in the Alex Student League activities. This made normal attendance at school difficult. Even police on the beat for crimes such as murder and robbery began to ask questions about student leaders. The peri-urban auxiliary police who were on the West Rand payroll to deal with housing permits for tenants were also on the lookout for troublesome student leaders. Community members would warn us that someone they knew working for these entities was asking questions about Black Power ringleaders. The Alex Student League resolved to be always on the alert and try as much as possible to be a step ahead of the system by not staying at home.

We manifested our influence in all the schools, from the primaries to the coloured school on 2nd Avenue, by briefing the school principals and teachers on our programmes. I was responsible for Bovet Higher Primary on 16th Avenue. The principal was Mr Simon Matlou, our next door neighbour in Tembisa. The Matlous had also been our 5th Avenue neighbours, and, like us, had been forcibly removed to Tembisa. My discussion with him was obviously awkward, yet we discussed the situation openly. I was not going to disrespect his authority at the school. I had always shown deference to adults like him, who had seen to my development over the years.

The ASL leadership was a formidable team. We tried hard to play the role of responsible young adults. We worked with university students residing in Alex, who provided guidance from the South African Students' Organisation. We read up on Black Consciousness positions and often quoted from the SASO newsletter. In 1977, the March edition focused on the memory of 21 March 1960, using pictures of the Sharpeville Massacre and depiction of those killed by the police as heroes of the struggle. The newsletter had a punch line: We Can't Stop Now.

All of us in the ASL were pushing the Black Consciousness line. We acknowledged that each of us had a prior preference for the PAC or the ANC, but we felt that Black Consciousness made the most sense to us. PAC stalwarts such as the school principal Rikhotso and Thabang's uncle (who told us of the Youth League influence in the ANC branch and the split in the Africanists who formed the PAC) suggested that we belong to Black Consciousness organisations, and not the PAC, because it was banned. The ANC, on the other hand, recruited openly from the student population, encouraging the exile route and the armed struggle. We tuned in to Radio Freedom. It was accessible on medium wave. The ANC propaganda machine was well oiled. In Alex at the time, they were the talk of the town, with the trial at the Old Synagogue Magistrate's Court in Pretoria involving a motley crew of operatives such as Jacob Kanakana Seatlholo of the Americans gang and a well-known bootlegger in the township, as well as others like Bam, who was said to be a state witness. The trial included younger activists, like Naledi Tsiki and Tokyo Sexwale and fourteen others.

The young women in the leadership were more militant and more fierier than the young men. Eunice Setati addressed a school community meeting, urging the students to take up where their freedom-fighter parents had left off. Her parents had been known Africanists in the structures of the liberation movement. We came to know her mother, who would arrange group lunches for us.

Benedicta Nomvume 'Tsotso' Maselana defied her grandparents after they had harangued her to stop engaging with struggle issues. They were shocked by the things the police told them their granddaughter had done, and threatened to deal with her once they found her. Tsotso sought refuge in the homes of her extended family and friends.

Tsotso arranged for her uncle, Linda Twala, who worked for the bus company Putco and dabbled in community work, would give us a private viewing of a feature film on the United States slave trade: *The Autobiography of Miss Jane*. The film starred Cecily Tyson. Again we found resonance with the black experience in the US. They had their Black Power movement, led by the likes of Stokely Carmichael.

Another of our number was Sipho Psypho, who had been doing a music degree at the University of Zululand when he was summarily expelled for participating in student strikes. He had a fantastic collection of rhythm and blues music and he was a huge fan of Curtis Mayfield, collecting all his available albums. At least we also had music.

The girls in the school gave the ASL attention and unqualified support. While we had younger boys becoming politically educated, the seniors were not amused. They didn't share our commitment to struggle politics. One of our campaigns was to entice the girls from the shebeens. The popular shebeen kings and their patrons did not like this one bit, especially when we burst in at night and volunteered to take schoolchildren home. Ours was a nation-building programme.

I was a late bloomer with girls. My first 'romance' ended when Lerato Kgasake asked me to end the relationship, largely because I had no time for her. The thrill of puppy love was gone. The possibility of making teen pregnancies was real, what with the schools not running as per normal. I played it safe. As a collective we were supposed to be upright leaders who could be trusted with the future of young people.

There was a lighter side, of course: the give-and-take banter among ourselves. Those who knew how to persuade a crowd of students into a hall were often entrusted with taking to the podium. Steve Tau was carefree and not very political. He was charming and liked speaking in public. He was also the only one among us who drank hard liquor. His input at leadership meetings was low. However, his ability to sway the mood at a meeting was extraordinary.

Another *broer*, Hlome Mbatha, was diplomatic. He could argue most persuasively in a crowded hall. Sylvester, on the other hand, was charming and articulate. He made it easier for people to comprehend difficult issues. For my part, I often made light of the difficult circumstances and used humour to make the schoolchildren laugh out loud. Thabang Makubire was good at figures. He calculated like a mathematician and often made the complex simple.

On one occasion, I was in a delegation led by Thabang to meet up with the SSRC, led by Trofomo Sono, at a secret venue in Orlando West. The tidal wave of the struggle was rising. What was significant about the meeting was that there was no certainty about what might happen next. Trofomo famously said, 'We will meet next in hell or heaven, or in John Vorster Square.' Trofomo's group had forced the community leaders to liaise with them and the authorities through the Committee of Ten, led by Dr Nthato Motlana. The Urban Bantu Councils, they were His Master's Voice.

The ASL created alliances with the parent group, the Save Alexandra Campaign, led by prominent community members such as Rev Sam Buti, Mme Gladys Serote, Harry Makubire and others. They were against the forced removals and displacement of families, and they campaigned against families being taken to City Deep in the south-eastern part of the city. They also raised the issue of the right to property ownership in Alex, where landowners with title deeds lost their properties if they were moved. The ASL arranged a petition against these removals. I was arrested by the West Rand Bantu Administration Board officials and taken to their offices in Wynberg. They called Rev Buti and he said what we were doing was in the best interests of the community. They let us be. I was severely criticised by my colleagues in the ASL, because if the authorities had handed me over to the Special Branch I would have been detained for a lengthy period.

As mentioned earlier, our school premises were derelict and in need of repair. The ASL decided to help repair the damage. We approached Dorkay House on Eloff Street and agreed with the manager, Peter Tladi, to stage a show where we could raise funds through the entrance fees. We also packed schoolchildren into Kings Theatre bioscope on 2nd Avenue, to watch *Casey Jones*.

We arranged for a showing of the feature film of Shakespeare's *Macbeth* at the same Kings Theatre. Unfortunately, the seats at Kings were full of bugs, and it was difficult to concentrate with bugs swarming all over you.

Our fund-raising efforts went beyond entertainment. We arranged with the manager of the Putco bus company for them to offer free transport to the funerals of students. We had burials to attend to. One was the death of Lovers Laban of 3rd Avenue, killed in a knife attack by my childhood friend Mallah. It was devastating. Lovers had been on trials with Kaizer Chiefs to play professional soccer. He was an outstanding football player with great promise. Alex was a death trap. I spoke on behalf of the ASL at his funeral. His brother Simi, also a football player, went on to join Highland Park Football Club when the race restrictions were relaxed in later years.

We also experienced violence among the students themselves. Sephuma was attacked with a knife by one of my former classmates, Johnny Makhathini. Johnny was a user of marijuana. Sephuma was a karateka. The attack was unprovoked. Sephuma had been asked to demonstrate his nunchaku skills against a knife attack. It started in the boys' toilet, where provocations often started on any subject. The groups using dagga as a form of recreation would go beyond the limit and start abusing other innocent male students. Johnny advanced with his jungle knife, despite Sephuma's protestation that he was not playing anymore. I saw this as it happened. We had to rush the injured Sephuma to the clinic.

A few days later, I was walking from the school premises when I was accosted by Oupa Kola carrying a self-made jungle knife and threatening to stab me. I had known Kola over the years. His eyes were bloodshot and he appeared inebriated. I took two steps backward, to decide whether to fight or flee. A bevy of schoolgirls was nearby, witnessing the incident. Gomolemo Radebe and her friend rushed over to stand between us. Another, Hodges, who was the class monitor in Joe Sefatsa's class, also rushed over to hold Kola back. It was only later that I realised I could have been stabbed to death that day.

Soon afterwards, a parallel group to the ASL was established by the mob contingent of the students. They called themselves the Alex Students Organisation. They wanted a full-blown fight with whites. They came to meetings drunk and generally misbehaved. We dismissed their arguments. We were not ready to have an all-out fight like that. Our main concerns were to secure a conducive environment for learning and teaching. We were also concerned with societal problems affecting black people, and the overarching struggle for national liberation.

It seemed our leadership was getting too sophisticated for our peers. We were said to be 'the situations', mocked by the locals for speaking in English and having answers for every question. Politics was an intellectual vocation for many. The anger around us was beginning to reach the level of calling for armed struggle. It was not a viable proposition, because we were unarmed, using only stones as weapons. I could not be persuaded at that time that moving in that direction would bear any fruit.

Our approach in the liberation struggle was influenced by Black Theology. We easily adapted our Christian upbringing to this interpretation of our oppression by a white-dominated oppressive regime. Sylvester often made us understand that he was praying to a living God. We were not engaging in platitudes on the nature of the struggle. We simply had to make progress incrementally and go on with preaching the gospel of Black Power.

Our plans to continue with teaching and learning at the high school were affected by the interference of the school board. The board took instructions without question from the Department of Bantu Education, and this brought them into conflict with teacher and parent associations.

Beyond the school issues, the Special Branch scuppered all the efforts for reconciliation we had initiated between the victimised shopkeepers and the community. We realised the need to differentiate ourselves from the tsotsi elements who looted from the shops each time social unrest took place. The Special Branch went for the jugular, hunting for the student leadership, and we had to flee the township. Sylvester and I went to stay with his aunt in Winterveld, outside Pretoria, for two weeks.

Our frustrations with returning order to the schools were getting the better of us. At an executive meeting in August, we heard that the *Rand Daily Mail* had reported that Robert Sobukwe, the banned leader of the Pan Africanist Congress, whom I had always admired, was sending his two children off to the United States to further their education. This definitely got my goat. I was fuming about leaders who looked after their own interests first, when we, the children of poor folk and the leaders of the students' struggles, were deep in the mire, with no solution to our predicament at hand. The executive committee was not impressed with me attacking a national leader. At seventeen, I was the youngest in the leadership team, so when times were tough, I was the most prone to displays of emotional displeasure and senseless talk when times were tough. I stood my ground. This open display of privilege for the leadership was deeply discouraging, I insisted.

I refused to apologise. This was the stone in me. It was also my boyish high-school anger, I later came to realise.

The year 1977 was a tumultuous year in the struggle: we gained ground, suffered defeat because of arrests and deaths and those skipping the country. Many leaders were summarily detained under Section 6 of the Terrorism Act or laws enabling indefinite detention without trial. One of the teachers, Cindy Radley, was taken in under such laws. It was the second year in a row that we had experienced a winter of discontent.

By now I was increasingly devoting time to writing, to poetry mostly. About this time I met Nunka Mkalipe, a stringer for *The World*. He was related to Super Sipho (the history teacher Sipho Zungu), and we became acquaintances. He backed our student struggles. I told him I wanted to write for the newspapers one day. I could feel it in my bones that I was destined for writing. He laughed it off, but said that if I wanted to join the trade I should know that it came at a price. I didn't understand. I thought he probably meant I'd need more schooling before I could attempt to write for the public.

I told my cousin Lillian that I was going to have my name in the newspapers every day as a journalist. It was a solemn promise, a covenant with a dear beloved cousin. My desire was based only on what seemed to me an inborn talent, waiting to be developed.

In the ASL we had latent talent. Mindlo Cebekhulu was in the Tembisa X1, a football side that played on Sundays against professional teams like Orlando Pirates and Kaizer Chiefs. They said he was like Des Backos, a white player in the National Football League. Sylvester's father was a boxing enthusiast and chaired the Orlando Pirates branch in Alex. Obed Bapela was a devoted Lutheran Church youth activist. Louis Mametse saw himself becoming a businessman in the coming years, like his elder brother who ran a taxi line between Tembisa and Alex. We all had dreams to fulfil.

Lindi Mnyele held a birthday party at her father's African Methodist Episcopal Church premises one Saturday afternoon. I was awkward with girls my age. We danced to American black music by Motown artists such as Stevie Wonder, Diana Ross, Nina Simone, Donny Hathaway and others. The black artists in the US resonated with us.

But while these things were happening, the political programme started to dictate our activities. As leaders, we almost immediately identified the school grounds as a battlefield against the Bantu Education laws. And we took our struggle to the teaching fraternity and the education authorities, such as the school board in Alexandra. We criticised the teacher-pupil ratio as deliberately designed to make the workload for teachers burdensome and to leave behind learners who were struggling with lessons. We questioned the lack of suitably qualified teachers. The government system admitted people without matric certificates as teachers, and let them teach Form 5 classes. We decried the expensive school fees and equally expensive textbooks. In essence, the Bantu Education system was interested only in pushing us out in to an economic system that had no room for black people other than as cheap labour. we saw the expansion of the homeland system as an adjunct to apartheid schooling and the ultimate destination for black people. But we had been born in urban areas, as had been our parents. Apartheid meant that our lives as we knew them were no longer going to be the same.

Weeks later, on 12 September 1977, Stephen Bantu Biko, the honorary president of the Black People's Convention and founding member of South African Students' Organisation – a leading light in the Black Consciousness Movement – was reported to have died in detention. It was clear now that the predators in the Special Branch were killing at will. Raids by the police were intensified. We had to lie low.

Steve Biko had gained prominence in our circles when he gave defence testimony in the SASO trial in the Pretoria Magistrates' Court. Even though he could not be quoted in the media, the journalists wrote that he was articulate in his defence of the Black Consciousness philosophy of struggle. The court hearing was well attended. Winnie Kgware, a BPC leader, also led the sessions in song before the judges came in. The SASO/BPC trialists were charged with treason for staging celebratory rallies in support of Frelimo and Mozambique's independence in 1974. They were sentenced to prison terms and became heroes of the struggle.

The next month, on Wednesday, 19 October 1977, all the Black Consciousness organisations were banned. This included *The*

World newspaper and church organisations such as Pro Veritate (led by the Reverend Beyers Naudé of the NG Kerk). The jails were full of political detainees. Vorster, the apartheid prime minister, was ferocious in his response to the struggle efforts in the black communities.

However, there were cosmetic changes in response to our resistance. For example, the Department of Bantu Education became the Department of Education and Training. Some petty apartheid laws were repealed. The Urban Foundation, a nongovernmental organisation backed by the mining moguls, advocated improved housing for the urban workers, based on a mortgaged ownership plan that would run over twenty years, financed by the banks.

All these announcements came in rapid succession, to quell concerns over the suppression of protest organisations and the detention of many activists detained without the option of facing charges. There were also trials of the banned organisations. The Pan Africanist Congress of Azania, with its leaders, faced charges dating back to 1963. The leaders of the Soweto Students Representative Council also faced charges of treason and sabotage. These reports engendered a sombre mood in young activists like me. What were we to do?

In anger and in protest, we organised a 'pen-down' campaign against writing the end-of-year examinations for all schools in Alexandra: the primary schools, higher primary schools, the coloured school, and the high school. It was an emotional decision that arose in response to the apartheid state's brutal reaction to pupils. We felt, in our anger, that this was the right response.

Yet we had unwittingly painted ourselves into a corner. The education authorities turned all community-controlled schools into state schools. They simply centralised control of the education system and prepared for the new year.

In my discussions with Louis Mametse, a member of the ASL leadership, it was agreed that there was no way we could go back to class and take Bantu Education instruction. We would be seen as two-faced. We could not condemn a system and still allow ourselves to play a role in it. We would be collaborating with the apartheid system in the same way that the 'independence' of Bophuthatswana was, and in so doing, increasing the oppression of black people. The newly established homeland's independence meant that all people who spoke Setswana by virtue of their parents were now citizens of this new country. This was ridiculous. I was in a quandary. I had never been to the rural areas labelled as Bophuthatswana on the map. Yet, once the sham independence was declared, I had to have a travel document as my identity book because I no longer belonged to South Africa. Louis and I, with our Setswana-speaking parents, were caught between a rock and a hard place.

My teacher friend, John Mametja, who worked at Dr Knak Higher Primary, which was linked at that stage with the Lutheran Church, updated me on new policies aimed at ferreting out the ringleaders of the uprising and barring them from attending the schools. Effectively this cut those of us in the leadership of the Alex Student League out of the education system. At the same time, our homes were being raided by the Special Branch.

A fellow pupil in Standard 9 at Musi High School in Pimville, Elias Lee Modiga, alerted me to the formation of the Soweto Students League to plug the gap left by the banning of the SSRC. The last leader of the SSRC, Trofomo Sono, was in exile with the Pan Africanist Congress of Azania. Lee and Collin Kotu, another Soweto Students League leader, were soon detained and faced charges that led to their conviction and a five-year spell on Robben Island.

7

Under the Guise of a Book Club

We needed to keep up the struggle, but things were going badly for the Alex Student League. Hlome's girlfriend had fallen pregnant, so he was working at a supermarket to earn money. Obed Bapela was working for the ANC underground. Together with his girlfriend Constance, they worked with the pupils at Alexandra High to keep our protests current. The rest of the others were steadily getting sucked into the humdrum of daily life. I did not want to join them. I felt I had a date with destiny. Our mission was to bring down apartheid and end the exploitation of black people.

Being activists under the surveillance of the Security Branch, going back to school was not a viable option. Sure, I could have gone to school in a rural area and probably escaped detection, but that would have been to betray the trust and support of all the young people who had missed a school year. I thought about registering at Turret College (an adult-education facility) to upgrade my matric to a university entrance certificate. Alternatively, there was also a correspondence option with Damelin College. The issue that was uppermost was how that would differ from Bantu Education. Whichever way I went, the decision would be political.

One of the biggest branches of the banned Black People's Convention was in Tembisa, and its strongest base was in my area, Moteong. On that fateful day in October 1977, when so many organisations were banned, a well-known figure in my neighbourhood, James Moleya, was also detained at Modderbee Prison near Daveyton on the East Rand. Through his family we got to learn about the appalling conditions under which people were being detained. Most of the *smallanyana* boys, as they were called then, were from my generation or were BPC members who had been recruited to participate in this Black Consciousness organisation when the 1976 uprisings gained momentum.

One day Tlhaki Lekganyane and Alex Mogale Segale visited me at home to suss me out politically. I held my own. They were also in the BPC. We spoke about the politics of resistance in the aftermath of the October 1977 banning and what was going to happen to the Black Consciousness Movement. I was for expanding work with the underground structures of the PAC and ANC. The generation gap in the struggle had to be narrowed. They invited me to Mogale's home. Mogale had matriculated from a boarding school in Thaba Nchu, in the Orange Free State. Tlhaki was unemployed, although he had once worked for some companies in the Isando industrial site. Both of them were convinced of the relevance of the Black Consciousness Movement. Apart from that, we all enjoyed jazz.

Our discussions were about advancing the struggle. I suggested we form a book club to exchange information and to mobilise others. We drafted a constitution and formed the Babopi Book Club. Of prime importance was to circulate banned books about the resistance movement, although I read anything of interest, from fiction to political books. There would be no more fluff.

We enrolled all the BPC members in the book club. My responsibility was to get access to books.

On the wider stage, at the end of February 1978, Robert Mangaliso Sobukwe died. There had been reports of his ill health since the death of Biko five months prior, but his death still came as a sad blow at a troubled time. To fill the vacuum of leadership at the national level, the Action Committee of Six had been established. Ishmael Mkhabela, Lybon Mabasa and Zakes Mofokeng were on the committee, and I went to see Zakes to find out what plans were being made. He was then assistant manager of the new ecumenical weekly newspaper, *The Voice*, based in Braamfontein. He told me that the committee was going to form a new national political organisation, and I would be his contact for Tembisa. There was also to be a prayer service for Sobukwe at Diakonia House, across the road from the newspaper offices.

On the day of the service I happened to be sitting next to Mothobi Mutloatse, a senior journalist at *The Voice*. After the service – incidentally conducted by Reverend Peter Storey, Sobukwe's spiritual leader – I introduced myself to Mothobi. I knew that he encouraged poets to submit their work to him, so I took the opportunity to ask him to read some of my writing. He did so then and there and said he'd place it in his Loud and Clear column in *The Voice* in the coming edition. I told him about the Babopi Book Club, mentioning that we needed books. He told me that the United States Information Service could help with books by black authors in the US. He had returned at the end of 1977 from six-month writers-in-residence programme at the University of Iowa in the States. Back in his office, he treated me as if we were long-lost friends. I noticed a collection of essays by various writers on his desk, and asked to borrow it for a week. In his dry way, he emphasised that the title of the book was 'Bring Me Back to Mothobi'.

At the time he was collating the writings of Casey Motsisi, a *Drum* columnist who had passed away in 1977. His plans were to publish them with Ravan Press. I blurted out that publishing books with white publishers was questionable, given the censorship, warning that he would be forced to tone it down. I was, to be frank, talking of matters about which I hadn't a clue. In his quiet way, Mothobi told me about a new literary magazine that Ravan Press was publishing with the intention of providing an outlet for younger writers. He suggested that I introduce the book club I represented to Ravan Press. There were opportunities galore for creative groups in the townships.

I went back to Tembisa with springs in the soles of my takkies. Firstly, I wanted to arrange a commemoration service for Robert Sobukwe in Tembisa. We could not turn our backs on this intellectual giant and leader of the African people. The PAC shared much of the thinking of the Black Consciousness Movement, and as advocates of Black Consciousness we could not dissociate ourselves from Sobukwe's organisation.

I suggested to Tlhaki and Mogale that we organise a memorial at the local high school. With the support of the school headmaster, Ralph Mothiba, himself a member of the now-banned BPC, we held a service a few days later in the school hall. Mogale and I addressed the meeting, which we held during the afternoon study hours. I was an awkward public speaker in spite of my know-it-all attitude; nevertheless, I emphasised equal rights for all in my speech and identified Sobukwe as a champion of those rights. I challenged my contemporaries to be like Sobukwe and pick up from where he had left off. Mogale delivered a dramatic message. He wondered what would have happened if Sobukwe, Mandela, and other leaders had been able, in unison, to confront the Vorster government? He wondered what would happen if the youth did not take up the fallen spear and fight to the end? We made a big impression, apparently. Many of the students – some had been to Alex and knew of my student activities – came to us afterwards seeking more information and saying they were prepared to take instructions from us.

Afterwards, I walked home with Mogale. I told him I wanted to be as articulate as the Black Consciousness leaders. He quietly suggested that I had to learn to express myself and speak the English language confidently. Such things, he said, were learned over time.

Then the girlfriends of Mogale and Tlhaki both fell pregnant at about the same time, which meant both men had to find paid employment. This was a blow for me. The three of us had made a formidable team. They both loved listening to free jazz. Mogale paid attention to the lyrics of every song, listened to every instrument, analysed the melodies. We spent time discussing books, one of our favourites being *Soledad Brother: The Prison Letters of George Jackson*. We often wondered about the 'love in the revolution' romance Angela Davis had had with Jackson.

I followed up with the US Information Service and they contributed about 500 books and magazines to the club. These were mostly fiction, poetry, and drama by African American authors. We also had books on Malcolm X, Booker T Washington, Martin Luther King Jr, black history, United States administration structures, economic principles, and journalism, and even career guides. High school students borrowed books and never brought them back, but we knew they were being passed on. While we knew that the Information Service was a US government outlet established to inform young people about life in the US, we also knew that the Central Intelligence Agency was probably keeping tabs on those who visited the service's offices. For us, the US Information Service was attractive because it didn't discriminate on racist grounds, whereas the public libraries did, and made membership difficult. So the Information Service facilities became a place of activity and study for many of us.

I again met with Zakes Mofokeng and he arranged for me to be part of a delegation to attend a meeting in Roodepoort to discuss a new national organisation. In the event I wasn't able to attend, but two from the book club – Jowie Letsoalo and Sanza

Melaong– did. Soon after this meeting, Mofokeng was detained. So were Ishmael Mkhabela and Lybon Mabasa, who had arranged Sobukwe's funeral. The Action Committee was in disarray, with most of its members in indefinite detention under Section 6 of the Terrorism Act.

On a Wednesday morning in April, I approached Obed Musi, then a columnist and subeditor on *The Voice*, to convince him to write a story on Hlome Mbatha, who had been detained that morning. I had kept in touch with ASL leaders and had been feeding books through to Hlome. His mother had told me about the Special Branch raid, and I wrote up three paragraphs, which I gave to Musi.

In return I got a lesson in the basics of reporting news, and I learned that I must answer the five Ws: who, what, when, where, and why. He also told me to write in a conversational manner. I rewrote my paragraphs. Not only was it a battle with the words but a struggle with a typewriter, which I was using for the first time. I used a 'two-finger typing method' method with my index fingers. Once my rewriting efforts were complete, Musi told me the story would appear in the Friday issue. He then asked me to fetch a parcel from the offices of the Institute of Race Relations in De Korte Street. I was to hide it from his colleagues. I never checked the contents of the parcel, but I suspect it was a *mahog* – a half-jack of brandy.

This was how my career as a freelance journalist began. Over the next weeks, the experienced journalists and photographers helped me fine-tune my writing. At *The Voice* was a number of big-name journalists and photographers: Sekola Sello, Phillip Mthimkhulu, Juby Mayet, Mothobi Mutloatse, Carol Mathiyane, Mabu Nkadimeng, and Ralph Ndawo. They understood the black experience and reported on the uprisings and the bannings.

In addition to *The Voice* there was the *Post*, a major daily, with a growing black readership. Their reports were not about witchcraft and lowlife clashes in the townships and did not typecast the community as one without leaders or a political future. I took up the arts and entertainment beat for both newspapers.

This gave me an opportunity to interview actor John Kani, who told me about the early township days of the Serpent Players in Port Elizabeth. Their production of *Sizwe Banzi is Dead*, a duo with Winston Ntshona, was attracting mixed-race audiences and had extended its run because the bookings were increasing. He and Ntshona had jointly won the prestigious Tony Award for Best Actor. They had to walk a careful line between the cultural boycott and the value of the stories told by plays like *The Island* and *Sizwe Banzi*. It was this home-grown talent being given support and recognition abroad that made local audiences sit up and want to watch.

That interview with Kani was a milestone in my early steps in journalism. However, Obed Musi thought I could have done better, that the piece was pedestrian. He showed me other ways of writing the story and the devices journalists used to enhance their writing. Damn, I needed education and creativity in this game. His advice was to write in my own voice, as it also needed to be heard.

At another time, Phillip Mthimkhulu and Sekola Sello poked fun at me, accusing me of not being as productive as a freelancer should be. I had to decide if I was living or existing. If I lived I had to earn a living, and if I merely existed, I was doing the black experience a disservice. Even though this was said in jest, I took it seriously. Sello was a sports journalist and Mthimkhulu wrote topical stories, including politics. They were part of a new body set up to replace the banned Union of Black Journalists.

To return to the story of Hlome Mbatha: he was eventually released from detention, and after further harassment by the police, went into exile. Soon afterwards Thabang Makubire also skipped the country. We were all on the run.

I had already exposed myself by writing for newspapers and for *Staffrider*, a literary journal published by Ravan Press. I was also working with arts groups in the Witwatersrand townships, helping to promote poetry readings. This gave the arts a 'voice' in the communities, and our festivals packed the halls.

Matsemela Manaka was a name to reckon with in these activities. He was head of the Diepkloof Arts Association, and, on the strength of his matric certificate, was employed as a temporary teacher at his former school. He was an energetic and creative thinker, dabbling in painting, performance poetry, music, drama, and poetry.

At the time, Mike Kirkwood of Ravan Press was toying with the idea of both Matsemela and me co-ordinating arts groups to distribute *Staffrider* on a hand-to-hand basis. The first issue was banned as soon as the censorship board clapped eyes on it. We were certain that if we distributed two thousand copies fresh from the printers via this hand-to-hand channel, we could beat the censors.

Kirkwood, a former lecturer in English literature at the University of Natal, had taken up the position of publisher at Ravan Press when the previous publisher, Peter Randall, was banned and placed under house arrest on that fateful day, 19 October 1977. Randall had initiated the Spro-Cas series of books and published them under the Ravan Press imprint. Kirkwood was associated with academics such as Rick Turner, Fatima Meer, Omar Badsha, and others in the Durban area.

In addition to the organising that was being done to distribute *Staffrider*, a local chapter of PEN International was established, with Mothobi in the chair. Membership was available to all South African writers. I helped with publicity and issued statements on behalf of the organisation.

Babopi Book Club had made an impression in Tembisa and was a conduit for the distribution of books unavailable in the book shops. We also distributed *The Voice* at Germiston train station. There had been a brutal killing at that station when Mthuli ka Shezi, a Black Consciousness adherent from Tembisa, was pushed in front of a train by white railway officials. No-one was held responsible. Making people aware of our reality at that station was one way of fighting back.

In retrospect I wonder if the books we sold were really read. Certainly, though, under the guise of the book club, we were able to reach many people and mobilise them with struggle literature.

8

Devil Eyes

The handcuffs bit into my wrists. The man brought himself closer to me and stared threateningly into my face. His eyes were sky-blue, and through his spectacles they seemed to bulge, then retract and turn a greenish blue as he moved his head. I wondered if this was some sort of chemical reaction after those bolts of electricity had been shot through my body.

The man wanted answers that would confirm his understanding of reality. Then he grabbed my collar with both hands and pulled me into his face. All I noticed were the wet hairs on the backs of his hands as they touched my cheek. They were spiky. Then I noticed his heavy breathing, the whistle of it from his nostrils.

He turned to his helpers, the black cops.

'*Vertel hom in sy eie taal*,' he said to them.

I was stony silent.

Before me was the notorious Devil Eyes. Political activists went through his hands in Tembisa. They said he would beat you up first and ask questions later, when you were nice and intimidated.

They all said he was as savage in his torture of detainees as the character in the popular photo story series *Savage*. I had read *Savage* in my younger days, like other cheap titles which came out biweekly, such as *Mark Condor, Lance Spearman, She, The Mighty Thor*. They'd been absorbing and easy to read. But that was then; now I was in a close encounter with Willem Coetzee.

The electric-shock torture, the bolts which had run through me, felt as if they were still continuing. I grunted and ground my teeth instead of screaming out loud. There was plenty of screaming coming from a nearby room. I had a stubborn streak. They didn't call me Stone for nothing.

Sergeant Willem Coetzee of the Special Branch and his horde of policemen had rudely awakened us at my Moteong home in the ungodly early hours of a winter morning. They confiscated reading material, books, and magazines. They told my mother they were taking me with them for questioning.

In their interrogation room on the first floor of Rabasotho Police Station, they swiftly got to work. I was thrown to the floor, my legs bent, my handcuffed arms around my knees. They inserted a broomstick between my legs and arms. I had heard stories about this treatment: how they would swing their victims around like a helicopter until they were dizzy. But this didn't happen. Instead, an electric cord was plugged in and the live wire at the end was stuck to my arms with sticky tape.

Coetzee asked if my name was Jaki Seroke.

I didn't reply.

He switched on the electricity.

I was not going to give him what he wanted from me.

One of the black policemen held me while I writhed, attempting to free myself from the electric cord.

I screamed as Coetzee sadistically switched on the current again, this time for a longer period. He asked why I was distributing terrorist material to people in Tembisa. Yet I knew the books were not banned. He recounted my speech at the Sobukwe memorial and asked why I was an organiser for banned organisations. He questioned the poetry readings we held at St Matthews Catholic Church.

His questions came quickly and he did not wait for me to answer before shooting more bolts of electricity into me. My grunts became louder. I was ashen by the time they stopped. I suppose it might have been about 45 minutes later.

I was taken to an empty room and left there. At dawn they drove me back home and kicked me out of the van and left me at the gate.

After this brutal experience I consulted with attorney Shun Chetty and Millard Arnold, an African American lawyer. They made me demonstrate the electric-shock treatment. Priscilla Jana, an understudy attorney in Chetty's firm, then opened a file. They were the go-to legal firm for struggle activists.

After that consultation I walked to the offices of Ravan Press. Mike Kirkwood suggested that I write a detailed report of what had happened and tell others in the literary world what tremendous pressure we were under from the police. I gave him a chapter and verse account of the torture I'd experienced at the hands of Willem Coetzee and his goons.

In the following week we decided at an executive meeting of PEN International to write in protest to the head of the Special Branch. This letter stated that I was not running a clandestine operation and that if they needed to know my views, all they had to do was read what I had written. The statement further protested against censorship and police harassment of creative writers. PEN International had the support of all the established writers in South Africa, including Nadine Gordimer, Alan Paton, and the Afrikaans writers known as the *Sestigers*, who were opposed to apartheid.

Mike told me a few days later that he had received an overwhelmingly positive response from the broad community of South African writers, in sympathy with my situation. They condemned the confiscation of books from my home and they called for the intimidation to stop. Rosa Keet, a well-known Afrikaans poet, pledged to pay my membership dues to PEN International SA as a gesture of friendship. The Writers in Prison Committee at *Index on Censorship* in London wrote a letter of protest to the South African Police. Nadine Gordimer offered to pay my tuition fees for a skills-upgrade course in writing that I had started. International playwright Tom Stoppard had one of his plays on stage at the time, and the actors observed a moment of silence in solidarity with the creative arts in South Africa, mentioning my name, among others.

Mothobi then suggested we act on our own as black writers and face the might of the police state without the backing that PEN International provided. To this end, we spoke in support of banned writers such as playwright Khaya Mqayisa, author of the banned play *Confused Mhlaba*; Reverend Mzwandile Ebenezer Maqina, author of *Give Us This Day*; poets Vuyisile Mdleleni and Farouk Asvat; novelist Achmat Dangor; essayist Fatima Meer; and journalist Don Mattera. We brought their plight to the global community of writers, and this isolated the Pretoria regime and its police state.

There were tensions with white writers because our needs were not the same as theirs. We were unpublished, for instance. There were no outlets to nurture beginner writers. One writer, Mtutuzeli Matshoba, wrote stories in longhand in the middle of the night, which were well received by *Staffrider*'s readers. None of the writers I knew earned a living from their writing. They hustled other jobs to eke out a living. They all had challenges. To start with, we worked in overcrowded 'dog-kennel houses', as Matshoba called them. There was literally no room for the solitary task of writing.

Devil Eyes Willem Coetzee made several more midnight appearances at my place, but I was never there. My high school instinct to *tsotsobala* came to my rescue. It was ridiculous for me not to sleep at home, though, as I had not done anything unlawful. When Coetzee did find me one night, he complained that my writings had reached the desks of his superiors and how they did not like what I had to say. I told him he did not have to make late-night visits. I was not an outlaw. On that occasion he did not resort to physical violence.

I wrote about his visit and submitted it to the writers' circle. I had come perilously close to endangering my young life by taking an interest in books and developing a deeper knowledge of the liberation struggle. My confidence grew. I could contribute to the private discussions I held with leading Black Consciousness people and I could teach the less well-informed.

One of the people I was in touch with during this time was James Moleya. He had a considerable presence in the community. He had been detained without trial and then released, and once he was free he arranged an exhibition of the paintings he'd done in jail. The exhibition was held in the foyer of the Methodist church on Pritchard Street, Johannesburg. Moleya had links with people such as Hennie Serfontein, a journalist who had written extensively about the secret organisation of Afrikaner hardliners called the Broederbond. He also knew Reverend Beyers Naudé, who agreed to view the paintings clandestinely, since he was a banned person and restricted to his house in the northern suburbs. The members of the Soweto Committee of Ten all bought a painting. Despite this show of support, art critic Thami Mnyele found the works depressingly grey.

The energetic Moleya was also fond of driving around in the Witwatersrand townships to spend time in the shebeens with the struggle leadership. He once told me a story of how he'd been made to eat humble pie. He had gone to Zephania Mothopeng's house in Orlando West in 1976, soon after the uprisings, to tell Uncle Zeph about his disappointment that the PAC leadership hadn't supplied arms to the angry generation. He said he had given the old man a dressing down on the lack of fighting spirit in the lions of the 1960s who had now become lambs. For example, some of the PAC leaders were in the urban Bantu councils created under apartheid legislation as dummy institutions. These former PAC members and leaders were now working in collaboration with apartheid. One such person, in Moleya's estimation, was Lennox Mlonzi, who had led a march in Soweto in the anti-pass laws campaign in 1960. Moleya said that Mothopeng merely brushed aside his allegations of collaboration as the dust from the hurly burly of struggle, suggesting that Moleya should be patient. Although Moleya regarded the Bethal Treason Trial, in which Mothopeng was the first accused, as a major showpiece of the PAC's struggle activities, he preferred the ANC's style and modus operandi.

With Moleya, I then met with visiting playwright, Zakes Mda, who had written powerful stage productions that played to rave reviews. One of his plays, *We Shall Sing for the Fatherland*, depicted the internal contradictions, corruption, and iniquities within the fraternity of freedom fighters. We met briefly with him, but I can't remember what we discussed.

In March 1979, the Benoni Special Branch sent new officers to raid my place. I had continued spreading banned reading material, according to their Captain van Niekerk. He had a handwritten copy of the banned Freedom Charter and said that it had been found in my possession by the police during a previous raid. It really *was* in my handwriting, and the police were unrelenting. They wanted to nail me. I had a framed Ralph Ndawo picture of Robert Sobukwe neatly placed on the wall next to my bed, with Sobukwe's words below it: 'True leadership demands complete subjugation of self, absolute honesty, integrity and uprightness of character, courage and fearlessness, and above all, a consuming love for one's people.' When van Niekerk saw this he tore it down and shouted at me in anger: 'Revolutionary!'

9

In Possession of Banned Literature

On Saturday evening, 7 July 1979, the Special Branch came to arrest me. I was thrown into a cell at Rabasotho Police Station for the rest of the weekend, treated like a leper, isolated and not spoken to. I was given food once the next day. At court on Monday morning, I was remanded in custody at Modderbee Prison, with the common criminals awaiting trial. No-one in my family or among my friends thought of finding me among these miscreants, petty thieves, confidence tricksters, pass-law offenders, rapists and murderers. No-one in the police state knew how to classify me. I had been arrested for reading and distributing a piece of paper called the Freedom Charter, and to most of the police this was incomprehensible. What sort of crime was this?

Modderbee was a multistorey prison, confining the inmates in a cold concrete jungle.

While I was there, the leaders of gangster groups asked me about the freedom struggle and how I would make money from it. The gangsters belonged to roughly four groupings, including two of the Numbers gangs. The fraudsters and con men were from the 26s, the murderers and robbers from the 28s. The petty thieves and collaborators with the prison authorities were from the Big Five, and the ones with a propensity to escape were called the Air Force. The 28s liked violence and fighting among themselves and with other prisoners. The fraudsters could talk themselves out of any situation. They lied through their teeth, saying that they used a 'statement' or 'machine' to get anything they wanted. The collaborators were sell-outs of the first order, eavesdropping on conversations and reporting to prison warders and the police in return for favours and extra food.

None of these groups could understand why I was categorised as a 'dangerous prisoner'. They had been warned to avoid me at all costs. At the end of each day, when the senior warders counted us to ensure no-one had escaped, I was asked if I was ready for *kulukutu* – the isolation cells. I never responded. Because there was a belief among the prisoners that those who were incarcerated in the isolation cells went mad, many of the gang bosses tried to persuade me to join their gang. I was given gifts of smuggled portions of pork or excused from cleaning duties.

Even though I had heard that it happened in prison, among common criminals mostly, I did not witness sodomy and was never accosted. Perhaps I was lucky, or perhaps there was a secret society that indulged in that behaviour.

I tried without success to get word to my family of where I was imprisoned. After eighteen days I was back in court at the Kempton Park Magistrate's Court, but this time my attorney, Priscilla Jana, was there. She got me out on bail. Neither the police nor the prosecutor apposed her application for bail. I don't remember what the bail amount was, but it took a while for the process to be completed and I had to wait in the cells until the paperwork was done. I walked out into the arms of my family and friends. My sister Ntlotleng was the first one I saw and I could not hold back tears of joy as we embraced. I was out in the blazing sun. Free. Interestingly, among my friends were Mothobi Mutloatse and Mabu Nkadimeng, keen to write up my story.

In the following weeks I prepared for the trial under the guidance of Priscilla Jana. She was continuing the work of Shun Chetty after police harassment had forced him into exile. Funding support for the trials of political activists came from the International

Defence and Aid Fund. Jana arranged for advocate Eric Dane to lead the defence.

My poor mother was under pressure from her friends in the township to consult a shaman who could influence events. As a family we had never consulted inyangas for muti or other dark-magic potions. In fact we were often criticised for our lack of traditional knowledge, not that this bothered us. And I could certainly not agree to a meeting with an inyanga.

The weekend before the trial, my mother pleaded with me to attend the Zion Christian Church service in Tshepo on the Sunday, which was the day before the trial began. This time, I compromised. I felt that should I be found guilty, she would be blamed for not taking proactive steps, and the guilt would be an albatross round her neck while I was in jail.

Mysticism was a topic I had discussed at length with other artists. Turn everything into a myth, make it larger than life – miraculous – place it in the celestial heavens where no mortals dared to tread, ascribe the outcome to the mysterious force of a supreme power, and whatever happened was beyond your control. But I could not believe in these forces; I needed evidence, proofs, scientific answers that could be analysed.

When the church service was over, I stood in a queue with my mother's church friends, waiting to be blessed by the priest. It was a long queue. Eventually my turn came and he listened to my story, then prayed for a while and told me to take a bottle of Coca Cola with me to court and I would be cleared. It seemed that there were people in my circle who were working against me.

I duly bought a bottle of Coke the next day and drank all of it before the trial started. We then went into the court.

Eric Dane had prepared well, and he used my writings on the torment and harassment that the Special Branch had meted out to me as part of his argument. He contended that I was being singled out for special attention by the Special Branch for no apparent reason. I was being intimidated, and this intimidation was intended to silence the creative-writing fraternity.

I had great support during the trial. Nadine Gordimer sat with my mother, and a furious Sipho Sepamla insisted he be allowed into court without a jacket. He was wearing a dashiki shirt, and the orderlies told him this was inappropriate attire for court. He put up such a row that they let him in to keep him silent. I was overwhelmed by the support I received from other established poets and writers as well.

Needless to say, the case was conducted in Afrikaans, but this was no problem for me.

During his cross-examination of van Niekerk, Dane ran rings around him. He brought up the police harassment, the electric-shock torture I had endured, and the lies and false material that had been used to implicate me in wrongdoing. During a break in the trial, the Security Branch consulted with their superiors and then went into negotiations with my defence team. There must have been some horse-trading, because the magistrate found me guilty but suspended the sentence. I would not do jail time, but I did have a nine-month sentence suspended for five years hanging over my head.

During all this, I had started to work on a full-time basis at Ravan Press. As a political activist, my chances of getting employment in a business or a factory were negligible, since these organisations were conservative and wanted law-abiding staff.

Joining Ravan Press was an ordeal. I was accompanied by the activist Glenda Webster to Esibayeni, in Albert Street, Johannesburg, to register for employment. My identity document was a travel document issued by the sham Bophuthatswana homeland. Even though I had been born and bred in Alex, I was lumbered with a 10(1)A status, which meant I had to leave the Witwatersrand

Clockwise from top right: me, Joe, Mike, Motheketlela (a neighbour's child), Mapule, and Tebogo Mohlafase. Taken in Alex in 1972.

LEFT:
Ntlotleng and me. Taken at Photo Hellas in Wynberg.

BOTTOM RIGHT:
At the Ravan Press offices, 1981, with unkempt hair. Defying conventionalism.

BOTTOM LEFT:
At Skotaville Publishers, explaining the decision-making process before a manuscript is accepted for publication.

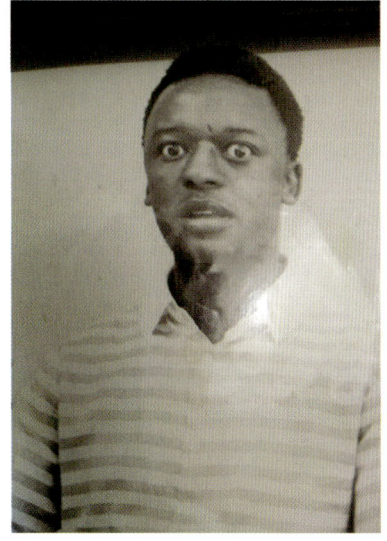

With my siblings. Clockwise from top centre: Ntlotleng, me with a trash photo story book in my hand, Mapule, Lucky, and Joe.

TOP:
Me on my confirmation day (left), with Mma Joe (my mother), Mme Sinah (my grandmother), Mme Sinah's friend, Mapule and Shimaboy.

LEFT:
In khaki clothing, emulating Robert Sobukwe.

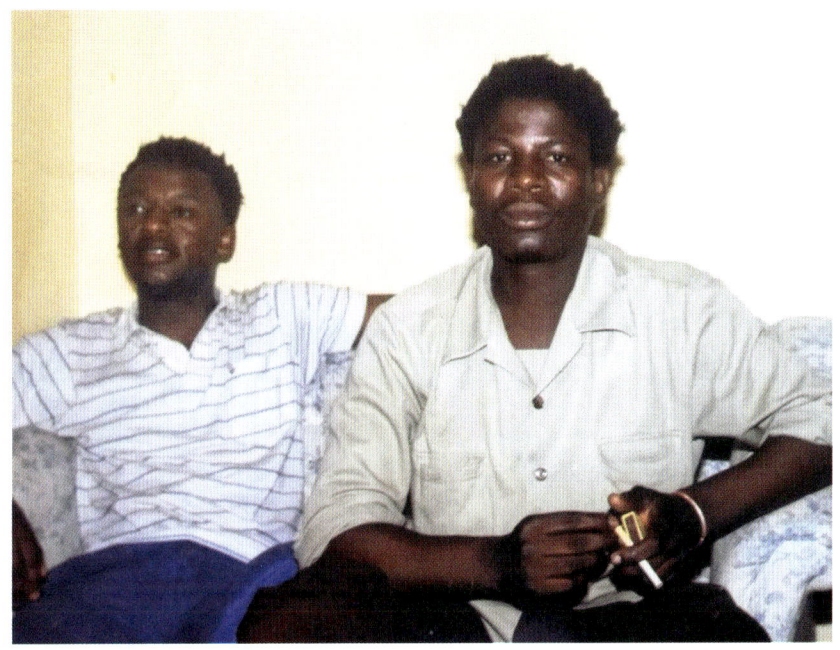

With Mafube Arts Commune's performance poet Maropodi Mapalakanye.

The car I used and was arrested in at the Koster roadblock. From police files.

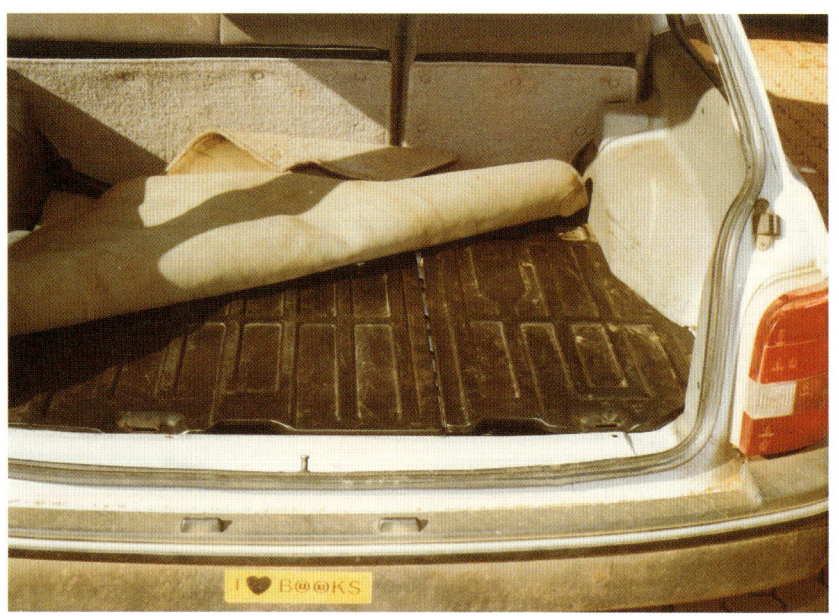

TOP:
The boot of the car had a false bottom, which was discovered and investigated by the police at the Koster Police Station. From police files.

LEFT:
The arms cache in the car. From police files.

BESTIGING MAR 9/238 NYP

BEELING C.R. V A K BR 278/87

DANIEL ABRAHAM BEKKER VERKLAAR ONDER EED IN AFRIKAANS:

Ek is 'n Kaptein in die S A Polisie verbonde aan die S A Krimi-
nele Buro, en gestasioneer by die P V A K Rustenburg as 'n Ap-
telike tekenaar en fotograaf in diens van die R S A.

Op 1987/09/10 het ek 'n voertuig, ligblou Ford Sierra stasiewa reg.
no NYP 659 T tesame met sy inhoud te S A P Koster, gefotografeer.

Dit behels foto's 1 tot 14 soos aangeheg.

Die voertuig met sy inhoud was aan my uitgewys deur Majoor Grobler.

Ek is vertroud met die inhoud van hierdie verklaring en begryp dit.
Ek het geen beswaar teen die aflegging van die voorgeskrewe eed nie.
Ek beskou die voorgeskrewe eed as bindend vir my gewete.

_____KAPTEIN
(D A BEKKER)

Ek sertifiseer dat die verklaarder erken dat hy vertroud is met die
inhoud van hierdie verklaring en dit begryp. Hierdie verklaring
is beëdig voor my en die verklaarder se handtekening is in my teen-
woordigheid daarop aangebring te Rustenburg op 1987/11/02.

_____
KOMMISSARIS VAN EDE
FRANCISCUS HENDRIKUS CORNELIS PLEISCH
P V A K PLEINSTR 153A, RUSTENBURG
ADJ OFF
S A POLISIE

The affidavit by the police photographer concerning the findings and photographs of the material found in the car. From police files.

Newspaper reports on the PAC/APLA trial in 1988.

area after 72 hours if I wasn't registered to work for a company. Being a loafer was a crime.

At the registration office, the white official in a khaki dustcoat sitting behind a desk took my forms without a word and indicated for me to unzip my trousers. I did not oblige. He called out to a black man, who told me to take my trousers down because the white man wanted to see my penis.

'For what good reason?' I retorted.

'If you want a job, do as he say,' the man replied.

What options did I have? I unzipped. I was humiliated and embarrassed. The white man entered his findings on the documents and gave them back to me. I took them to a clerk who stamped my employment registration, and I was now officially allowed to work for Ravan Press. I had a blue card for unemployment benefits. I did not tell Glenda about my excruciating experience; it was too much to reveal the indignity.

I took my first salary straight to my mother after cashing the cheque. It was R394.00. She gave me enough to buy a monthly train ticket and a small amount of cash to spend as I wished. The next month I told her she could stop working. Fifty per cent of my salary was more than she brought home for all her troubles. Now that I was earning a living, I could save her from being paid slave wages by her 'madam'. I have given her half my earnings ever since.

The editorial collective at *Staffrider* believed in a socialist ethos. We worked without a set schedule of hours. If working into the night was required, which at times it was, then that was what we did. It was called flexitime. We sometimes had to work over weekends.

On the team were Biddy Crewe, who took photographs and helped with the layout, and Andy Mason, who was responsible for graphic design and layout and was the practical clown in the team. He liked pranks and made jokes all day and night. Matsemela worked with the arts groups to gather their contributions. I co-ordinated the contents, read the proofs with author Rose Zwi, and liaised further with Kirkwood. I was on a learning curve, getting training on the job.

Biddy and Andy took me on the whites-only buses to their homes. No-one complained. Biddy was British and she loved mocking racialism in public places. White madams and their maids in uniform used the bus because the maid was on baby-care duty, and these were ripe pickings for Biddy. She was a feminist, concerned to get women emancipated from patriarchy. Although feminism was a hot issue, it was not high on the agenda of national oppression and anti-imperialism. I was interested in Biddy's opinions because women could mobilise a large part of society. To this end, I read Sheila Rowbotham's *Women, Resistance and Revolution*. She championed women's liberation.

Matsemela was an outspoken and independent-minded playwright with a public profile. He'd been interviewed by many newspapers regarding his views on theatre and the arts. He was described as a whizz-kid by the *Sunday Express*. His *Egoli* drama, a two-hander, was doing the rounds in informal theatres, until he was taken on by the Market Theatre, which was attracting new audiences with the struggle-related plays being staged there. The white left and liberals were paying attention.

We formed a formidable team at *Staffrider*, increasing circulation via a vast distribution network including the arts groups and alternative bookshops. We had also made the content more reader-friendly.

A grouping of critics formed an alternative to *Staffrider*, called *Wietie*. That was flytaal for a call to dialogue. Fhazel Johennesse and Chris van Wyk were the editors, and their main gripe was the seemingly low literary standards and lack of strong editorial control at *Staffrider*. The magazine petered out after two issues, mainly because of a lack of funding. Their underlying concerns were the deep-seated ethnic influences among the oppressed in the apartheid-controlled environment. In fact there was no escaping the effects of apartheid. For instance, the privileges accorded to Indians and so-called coloureds raised their ugly head in the growth of the *Staffrider* literary arts movement. The contempt among these people for indigenous Africans was almost tangible. The atmosphere was thick with this attitude towards African people, because the system encouraged it.

By way of example, Chris van Wyk published a volume of poetry with Ad Donker, entitled *It is Time to go Home*. The rave reviews in liberal establishments encouraged his version of literary politics, which were in contrast to the anti-establishment rhetoric of the new black protest contributions. Unfortunately, what ever progress was made inevitably suffered from push-back from such opponents.

10

The Art of Activism

My interest in literature and art developed tremendously during my time at Ravan Press. I became involved in the crucial debates about the value of art in society and, by implication, in the liberation struggle. I encouraged writers to put their blood, sweat and tears into creating texts for the national liberation struggle. I now had a purpose and a focus point.

Various friends and comrades, such as Thamsanqa (Thami) Harrison Mnyele and Nape 'a Motana, supported me in these efforts. Nape, a social worker, had been hounded out of Tembisa by Willem Coetzee after he launched Mihloti Arts Association and taught creative writing in workshops for young people. Mnyele lived in Emangweni Section with his wife Naniwe and their baby. I spent most of my time with them because we shared the same values, and we discussed these same vexing matters into the night. Matlhakanye (Thlaki) Joseph Lekganyane and Alex Mogale Segale joined the circle and we began to link politics and arts. Tlhaki had a deeper knowledge of the musicians and, as I've said, a decent collection of free jazz. Mogale connected the music to the struggle.

We developed into an avant-garde type of jazzophiles. It was not enough to listen; we read everything we could about this genre of jazz, from the liner notes to *Downbeat* magazine. It was an elite movement in the development of jazz that went against the prevailing trend of bebop, swing, and other mainstream music for the masses. Free jazz had the most talented artists, led by, among others, John Coltrane, Ornette Coleman, and Archie Shepp. Thami, with his vast collection of indigenous and non-commercial music, introduced us to amazing sounds, including the music of Dollar Brand, especially his popular album *Mannenberg – 'Where It's Happening'*. And then his wife was a powerhouse of insight into the songs performed by Miriam Makeba and Letta Mbulu.

Thami sat at his easel, painting, while the music played. Creativity inspired creativity. Nape wrote a poem inspired by Thami's work. Thami produced the cover art for three of Mongane Wally Serote's books: *Yakhal'inkomo*, *Tsetlo*, and *No Baby Must Weep*. He had also held art workshops at the Regina Mundi Roman Catholic church in Rockville, Soweto, for high school students. This was done under the auspices of the Music, Drama, Arts and Literature Institute, led by Molefe Pheto. Pheto was a founder member of the Medupe Writers Association, but was hounded out of the country by the Special Branch. The art classes were taught not only by Thami, but also with input from Ben Arnold and Fikile Magadlela, who'd both been inspired by the Black Consciousness Movement. Ben Arnold's most famous piece was a portrait of Sobukwe. Fikile made life-sized paintings of black men and women in robes reminiscent of Jesus Christ's era. Regina Mundi bought some of their pencil drawings and put them on public display in the church.

Meanwhile, the Vorster government was tightening the screws of suppression at every opportunity. The Action Committee convenors were summarily banned and restricted to their homes. Lybon Mabasa and Ishmael Mkhabela, who had organised Sobukwe's funeral in March 1978, then held a conference (which I attended as part of the Tembisa delegation) to launch the Azanian People's Organisation. The PAC was leaderless after the murder of David Sibeko and the death of Sobukwe. Vorster took to calling the PAC 'a monster without a head'. In the UK, the mission in exile faced a campaign by the Anti-Apartheid Movement to exclude them as representatives of the Azanian revolution. There were attacks against the organisation on all fronts. When a guerrilla of the Azanian People's Liberation Army died in a confrontation with the South African security forces in Soweto, the news of his heroic death never made the front pages or the news bulletins. Fortunately, the killing of Kenny Mkhwanazi was made known abroad by the PAC leadership. Unfortunately, however, factional battles plagued the liberation movement.

The African National Congress used the vacuum of leadership to assert itself once again. They took up a study tour that had first been offered to David Sibeko, revolutionary icon and representative of the PAC observer mission at the United Nations. Ho Chi Minh in Vietnam had invited the PAC through David Sibeko to Vietnam, to observe the successes of the communists and the Vietnamese people in their historic defeat of the monstrous imperial giant that is America. Instead, the ANC sent a delegation that included OR Tambo, Thabo Mbeki, and other senior figures. They came back with a strategy that became known as the Four Pillars of Struggle. A concentration of new and capable leadership advanced the core ideological position of the ANC as an internal front. This included an acceleration of armed propaganda conducted by uMkhonto we Sizwe, its military wing; the mobilisation of the international community; and the strengthening of the underground structures of leadership, including the long-term political prisoners.

It was in this stage of the revolutionary struggle that the debates on art and activism took place.

I had been reading a philosophical analysis of the meaning of art by Austrian Marxist Ernst Fischer. The book had made its way into the offices of Ravan Press and had been signed by Pitika Ntuli, the fine-arts graduate and teacher, who was now embroiled in the PAC's internal leadership squabbles. He was unceremoniously sent packing to London after being detained in Swaziland because he had been accused of being a co-conspirator in a marathon PAC trial being held in Bethal, out of the spotlight.

Fischer stated assertively that 'from a constantly growing wealth of evidence [we may conclude] that art in its origins was *magic*, a magic aid towards mastering a real but unexplored world. Religion, science, and art were combined in a latent form – germinally as it were – in magic. This magic role of art has progressively given way to the role of illuminating social relationships, of enlightening men in societies becoming opaque, of helping men to recognise and change social reality. A highly complex society with its multiple relationships and social contradictions can no longer be represented in the manner of a myth. In such a society, which demands literal recognition and all-embracing consciousness, there is bound to be an overwhelming need to break through the rigid forms of earlier ages where the magic element still operated and arrive at the more open forms – at freedom, say, of the novel. Either of the two elements of art may predominate at a particular time, depending on the stage of society reached – sometimes the magically suggestive, at other times the rational and enlightening; sometimes dreamlike intuition, at other times the desire to sharpen perception. But whether art soothes or awakens, casts shadow or brings light, it is never merely a clinical description of reality. Its function is always to move the *whole* man, to enable the "I" to identify with another's life, to make its own what it is not and yet is capable of being.'

My nineteen-year-old self took great comfort in this book. In my discussions with Mnyele, I also realised that some of the revolutionary leaders, such as Agostinho Neto, Samora Machel,

Mao Zedong, Aimé Césaire, Robert Sobukwe, Léopold Sédar Senghor, Kwame Nkrumah, and numerous others were also writers and poets of note.

Mnyele read Fischer's book too, and we talked over the subject some more. He reckoned that artists could play a greater role in the African revolution. I understood my role at Ravan Press as that of a cog in the wheel of the progressive forces of the world. These literary theories could be sharpened in the debates (both formal and informal), in the workshops, in the meetings) where concentrated focus was likely), and in formal academic studies of the theory of literature and art. I had found my purpose. I did not have to be academically trained to serve this purpose, but I had to acquire the skills required to lead. I had to add value to the struggle of committed artists and avoid being a doctrinaire ideologue with predetermined ideas.

Mnyele and I attended the launch of the Azanian People's Organisation' where George Wauchope chaired a most volatile session that showed how different were people's political ideologies. Of course, an important element was that we could have these debates at all, when the organisations were banned.

I sat at the back of the conference hall, next to journalists and activists Thami Mazwai and Joe Thloloe. Opposed in the debates were those who saw oppression as based on colour and land dispossession and those who saw it in terms of class and multiracialism. Another group, the champions of class struggle and trade unionism, was led by Curtis Nkondo and others I did not know at the time.

Mazwai was unremitting in his attack on the role of white liberals, the left academics, and the old-guard leadership who preferred useless struggle methods and co-operation with the settler regime. He was wildly applauded whenever he made a point. Thloloe was the chairman of the banned Union of Black Journalists and had been in detention for a long while after the June 1976 uprisings. Where Mazwai was outspoken, Thloloe was a conciliatory and unifying factor when matters went awry. At the conference, Mazwai declined the nomination for secretary-general, on the grounds of his journalist ethics. Curtis Nkondo was elected as president.

The various arts groups closely involved with *Staffrider* were beginning to define their roles. A group in Alex, Khawuleza, were leaning towards the leaders of the ANC in exile, while A Mofolo, a Soweto performance group, threw into their poetry the names of Nyakane Tsolo and Philip Kgosana, lesser-known leaders of the PAC. Ingoapele Madingoane was regarded by the black press as the poet laureate of the liberation struggle, with his powerful poem 'Africa My Beginning, Africa My Ending.' The *Staffrider* series published the epic poem 'Black Trial' and 'Africa My Beginning' as the main items of the poetry volume. The two thousand copies in the print run sold out in less than a month, before the censorship board had it proscribed. It was a time of art in politics, artists as political activists, and the art of activism all in one. We were living in interesting times.

11

The Fork Ahead in the Winding Road

While my political life was firing on all cylinders, my love life was in a shambles. I wasn't in a stable relationship, and the possibility of that happening was next to zero. My fears were that I would be attracted to an airhead, make her pregnant, and have to commit to marriage. I saw that happening to friends and comrades and realised that it would negate my political intentions.

Thami was an encouraging example. I would often tell him that his marriage was an inspiration. Something I aspired to have. A partner who could engage intellectually in matters of life and the national struggle. He laughed at my naivety. He must have thought I was a hopeless idealist.

He told me many amusing stories and true cases of individuals he knew who had been deeply hurt by love affairs. I insisted that I wanted the ideal woman.

'*Jy weet*,' he would preface his point, 'what you see is not what is real.' I was hopeless in these matters, he said, emphasising that it was only by getting involved with someone that I would learn the answers to my concerns.

Nape 'a Motana took me to be hopelessly young and inexperienced when I broached the topic with him. But then Faith Dimakatso Mofammere, a student nurse at Baragwanath Hospital and an art enthusiast, took my fancy. I dated her; we went to movies at the Lyric, Avalon, and Majestic, and for lunches in Fordsburg. We became great friends, and I truly loved her company and her philosophy of life. She had great ambitions. Most importantly, I was comfortable with her as a friend.

Writer Amílcar Cabral had said that it was not enough to be brothers in the struggle; we needed to elevate the relationship from brotherhood to comradeship. I believed that also in relationships, we needed to be more than just lovers.

I would visit Faith in Diepkloof every so often, at times taking Matsiks (Matsemela) and his girlfriend Nomsa Kupi with me. Nomsa was a modern dance student. She and Matsemela made a perfect love match in the arts.

Then his *Egoli* production was invited to West Germany. There they participated in the Erlangen International Theatre Festival and at the PEN International book fair. He went with two actors, John Ledwaba and Hamilton Silwane. The stage production had been tightened up with the help of Rob Amato, a protest theatre specialist. Matsiks found it hard to acknowledge the work done by Amato, though, because the *Egoli* story was an oppressed people's point of view.

Being in the editorial team at Ravan Press, Matsiks and I had read the collection of Steve Biko's writings by Father Aelred Stubbs, *I Write What I Like*. These had been written under the pseudonym Frank Talk in SASO newsletters and other Black Consciousness periodicals. Ravan Press was not in a position to co-publish the book at that stage, because most of the pieces by Biko had been banned by the state censors. We found Steve Biko's essays evergreen, however.

As Black Consciousness adherents, it was anathema for us to take tutelage from liberal white intellectuals. Matsiks' dilemma regarding Amato's contribution and improved stage production of *Egoli* was understandable, even the extent of Amato's advice was minimal, compared to the raw material that was in the play already. Matsiks saw this acknowledgement as insignificant. Amato, on the other hand, was furious.

In the creative industry, there were many issues of this nature, which were never resolved. Zacks Nkosi, of *Our Kind of Jazz* fame, often told his acquaintances that 'Mannenberg' was his composition, and that Dollar Brand had 'stolen' it from him.

Ravan Press's undeclared editorial policy was that team members would have to place their own creative writing work in abeyance and focus on helping would-be writers to produce high-quality work. It was a matter of putting the self aside in the interests of the bigger picture. I took Mike Kirkwood's approach of preferring to be in the background, selfless and unacknowledged, but doing work and producing books all the time.

Thami Mnyele was also caught on the horns of a dilemma. The amount of work he was doing for the ANC underground was getting serious, and it was exposing him to rats in the police surveillance system. We often talked about this without getting into details. He knew I was a staunch Pan-Africanist, attached to the PAC. We trusted each other because of the values we shared and the experiences we had gone through together. I wasn't hostile to the ANC, but I was angry at the critical way in which the newspapers treated the PAC. I often covered for him when he was out, over the weekend mostly, doing his underground work. I would never question him. He was often in Gaborone, as he had established contact with Mongane Wally Serote. Thami spoke perfect Setswana. He grew up in Makapanstad, an area of the Bakgatla-ba-Kgafela people in the north-western Transvaal. He was a disciplinarian – trustworthy – and took anyone's undermining of national commitment as a sacrilegious offence. This was also his approach to art. Attention to detail was everything. There were no grey areas as far as discipline was concerned. I had observed this attitude when our book club held sessions to discuss a book. Our originally big circle of participants declined because of the intensity of these sessions. In Thami's eyes, if you were going to do something, you did it properly.

Then he came up with a surprise. He called to tell me he was in a serious relationship with Rhona Segale, Mogale's sister. I couldn't understand this, but I couldn't judge him. Matters of the heart were personal, and words could not adequately express what was felt. I could not pretend to see things from his perspective. We remained friends, though, and I was pleased that he had told me himself, and I hadn't heard it from a third party.

Mogale must have known about this affair, as he had stopped coming to the discussions and music sessions. Tlhaki, equally, never said anything. We let the matter be.

As fate would have it, one summer afternoon I went to Thami's place but found no-one at home. He kept the house keys under a pot plant, so I let myself in and helped myself to tea and biscuits. It was peaceful to sit there alone, playing a selection of albums, from John Coltrane's 'Naima' and *Blue Train*, to Abdullah Ibrahim's *Tintinyana*; from Keith Jarrett's *My Song* to Tete Mbambisa's *Tete's Big Sound*.

While I listened, I read Arthur Nortje's poetry volume *Dead Roots*. His loneliness, disappointments, captivating images, longing for the sea – oh, the sea – in Cape Town were haunting. Nortje committed suicide in England. He was a most gifted black South African poet.

I slept over at Thami's, and the next morning went to the outside toilet. The bucket system was used in Tembisa. After my ablutions I went back to bed to continue reading. I have always read poetry slowly, trying to feel the poet's concerns and their ways of seeing, visiting the words again and again. Like appreciating a good painting on the wall, each time I go back to the words they mean something new to me.

Eventually Naniwe returned from her night shift at Tembisa Hospital. She made tea and we sat discussing her night's work. I described Nortje's life in his poems. I continued sipping my tea as she prepared to take a nap after her long night at work.

Then I heard her sigh heavily and leave the house in a hurry. About two hours later, out of curiosity, I went into her bedroom. On the bed was a note in Thami's handwriting, addressed to her: 'I regret to tell you this way. I've left the country for good. My work has been compromised and the movement has called me. Be strong.'

I knew exactly what it meant. Thami Mnyele had gone in to exile.

Naniwe came back with Thami's cousin. She was distraught, and kept herself in the bedroom, sobbing. It was the beginning of the end of their relationship. My model family. I was missing something. It was a fork in the winding road. Thami had determinedly resolved, without any pressure whatsoever, to go and serve his political organisation on a full-time basis. I respected that.

On the writing front, PEN International South Africa was rattled by differences of opinion within itself. The raw township style sat uncomfortably with some of the suburban membership. Even poetry readings were taking a tone that deliberately offended some members of the writers association. On one occasion at the Nunnery Theatre at Wits University – an event to launch some Ravan Press titles – there was to be a poetry reading as part of the programme. The performers came in traditional gear, dressed as warriors, and harassed and intimidated the daylights out of the mainly white audience, following an anticolonial theme.

These sporadic acts of guerrilla theatre were sometimes thwarted by the security agencies, and some of these freedom fighters were taken to the gallows, making the mainly black communities feel that they were under siege. The writers and artists merely conveyed their emotional appeal to be heard.

At about this time, Rose Zwi and I went to visit the banned Don Mattera at his house in Eldorado Park. His banning order had been relaxed to allow him to do subbing work at *The Star*. Rose was doing the rounds as a senior official of the organisation, meeting the banned writers. Mattera gave me his literary offerings to publish under pseudonyms. He used Monnapule Lebakeng (his mother's surname) and his Muslim name, Omar Ruddin. I made Rose aware of this. She was mentoring my editing and book-production management skills. Mattera continued to get unsolicited midnight visits from the Special Branch, and was kept under surveillance even at *The Star* offices.

Rose had been elected secretary of PEN International SA, with Mothobi the chairman, and I often issued media statements as a spokesperson. Rose occasionally felt put out by some of the controversial statements that we issued. She was mortified when a petition against the siege of Beirut was signed by many members PEN International SA after Ahmed Moosa launched a campaign. The petition was ultimately sent to the Israeli embassy. I issued a media release about it without consulting her. Except perhaps for Mike Kirkwood and Nadine Gordimer, the white authors could not grasp that harassment aimed at us was because of our activist standpoint against the regime, in addition to the writing project. We were openly resisting apartheid and settler colonialism. We were defying the culture of fear and silence. It was difficult striking a balance between the views of the white writers and those of the black poets and journalists. We came from two different worlds.

Some of the friends and comrades from the pre-1977 October banning days whom we worked with wanted to know how we could work with whites under these circumstances. The young and vocal women journalists working for *The Voice* did not mince their words. These were the likes of Belede Vabaza, Thembeka Mbobo, Ruth Bhengu, and Castalia Moleke, who saw the PEN International scenario as a betrayal of the core philosophy of Africanist thinking and Black Consciousness.

Mothobi and I met with a delegation of the Writers' Association of South Africa at the offices of the *Weekend World*. They were represented by Mandala Ndlazi of *Drum* and Joe Thloloe. They simply asked what had happened to us as Africanist/Black Consciousness adherents. Why were we in a power-sharing scheme with white liberals? Thloloe was blunt. Why were we in a unity of sorts between oppressors and oppressed? Mothobi gave an explanation, but the discussion deteriorated into cliches and rhetoric that pushed us into a corner. Thloloe had to pick up his school-going son in Orlando East in his VW Beetle. He gave us a lift and dropped us off in Pimville, at Mothobi's place. In the car the discussion was more relaxed and led to a better understanding among us. We were, after all, all comrades pursuing the same goal.

Other black writers, such as Es'kia Mphahlele, the doyenne of African literature, who kept himself at arm's length from the activities of the writers' community, had a different approach to the matters we faced. He did not advocate a split among writers. He said that we needed to focus on developing a conducive environment for more literary activity to arise from the African experience. His immense experience in teaching African literature in Denver and at other US universities was not properly utilised by us in PEN International SA. He gave well-attended public lectures at the Johannesburg public library on the culture and history of Africa. He was also appointed to teach at the Department of Comparative Literature at Wits University. He offered his services for continuing-education sessions for beginner writers and young community intellectuals.

I was at first not comfortable working closely with a returning exile, when many of my agemates were crossing the borders, running away from the security police. Mothobi suggested that we take the elder Mphahlele to Alexandra township for his first sightseeing visit since the 1950s. I was the tour guide. He was shocked at the level of poverty of the residents and the degradation and despair written all over the streets, as well as the donga that Alex had become for so many years.

In the first writers' workshop we held with him, Mphahlele pointed out that nineteen-year-olds still have a lot to learn in the development of their craft, and that they must not assume to know it all. The message sunk home. He cited texts from African writers to illustrate their weaknesses and strengths in writing. There was a crying need for writers' workshops.

As Dennis Brutus had described him in his poetry, Mphahlele was a sage.

Without any shadow of a doubt, we in PEN International SA were confronting a fork in the road. Mothobi, as chairperson, had to do something. Shortly after these revelations, a meeting was convened at the Market Theatre to discuss the quandary that most of the black writers felt they were in, regarding their close proximity to whites. They each talked agonisingly of their experiences and the feedback they received. The Natal group raised their dissent. Mafika Gwala saw this move as a betrayal of progress that had been made in handling the racial dichotomy. It was, however, a foregone conclusion that the Africanist and Black Consciousness viewpoint would prevail. PEN International SA was dissolved at that meeting.

12

The Struggle Continues

When we met to talk about our strategic objectives and tactical manoeuvres, our discussions were always robust. There were always contradictions, differences of opinion, and disagreements with one another, but this wasn't a bad thing. In fact, it enriched the debates. Politics is an inexact science and intellectual honesty is the best policy.

One of my favourite authors, Eduardo Galeano, admitted in later years that the language in his outstanding historical bestseller, *Open Veins of Latin America: Five Centuries of the Pillage of a Continent*, was stodgy and perhaps hackneyed. Since its publication he had improved his writing style, making it briefer and more exact. He conceded that he was not as educated then as he was now. This was in an interview that took place 30 years after the book was published. I valued his ability to be self-critical in public. Perfection is not of this world.

Some of the criticisms about the breakup of PEN International SA were sharp and ill-natured. Andy Mason and his friends, for instance, were called 'honorary blacks' for their calm response to the split. They were said to support Black Consciousness. However, Andy himself would unleash his wry humour and tell me to go find my Black Consciousness friends when I requested extra cash from him to take friends with me to Tembisa.

Mafika Gwala never minced his words. The split was ill-advised. He did, however, continue to exchange views with me on the broader political terrain. His point was that Black Consciousness was a transient phase in the liberation movement, while they reorganised to continue their missions. He was steeped in Muscovite perspectives. As far as I was concerned, Black Consciousness would need to spread far and wide among the masses who lacked self-esteem and feared their white masters. How do you rediscover your humanity when the ones in charge of the system responsible for your dehumanisation are telling you how to find your true self? *Haikhona!*

The dissolution of PEN occurred on a Saturday. The next day, in Diepkloof, we launched the African Writers Association. Es'kia Mphahlele had drafted the constitution, and after several changes and amendments, it was adopted. I was always on its committee, either as secretary, treasurer or organiser. The association was aimed at bringing the old and experienced and the young and new activists in the literary arts together.

The differences of opinion we had could not be defined as life-and-death. We had different approaches to the creation of a free and sane society. Even the levels of discussion were varied. But, crucially, the debates were nonantagonistic.

And then in the winter of 1980, the municipal workers brought Johannesburg to a standstill. The strike was about working conditions, wages, leave pay, and other emoluments that workers were entitled to under the new labour laws that had emanated from the reform recommendations of the Wiehann Commission in 1979. It was a strike led by activists who leaned towards the PAC. Thloloe was on the labour beat, covering the story. The Tembisa branch of the Azanian People's Organisation invited the secretary of the union, Phillip Dhlamini, to address one of its gatherings at the Lutheran church. He spoke from beginning to end in Nguni languages. He used phrases that could be associated with the Pan-Africanists. The PAC was once again coming to the fore.

In my office at Ravan Press one Saturday morning, a worker in a hard hat and overalls came looking for political books he could send home to a Transkei village for his son to read. I recommended *Black Politics in South Africa Since 1945* by Tom Lodge. He asked me for its contents in brief. After listening attentively, he agreed to buy it. I would have thought it an expansive purchase for him, but he didn't quibble. He asked what else I would recommend.

He then said to me, 'I was once on Robben Island for the activities of Poqo [the armed wing of the PAC]. I followed Sobukwe. Not Mandela.' He wanted his son to be well-informed in politics.

It was getting interesting. I showed him the political titles and Ravan's labour series. Most of the titles were by researchers at Wits University and other institutions. There were no black political analysts published by Ravan Press at that time. I had copies of *Ikwezi – a Journal of South African and Southern African Political Analysis* on the Ravan Press shelves. Bennie Bunsee, its editor, who was based in London, had been sending me copies regularly. I gave the Poqo man two editions at no cost. He took them and we shook hands. 'Thank you, son of the soil.' It was the first time someone had called me that, and it felt good.

Meanwhile, things were moving in my personal life. I had fallen for a student at the University of the Western Cape, Terry Matthews. I had never seen such beauty before. We were equally attracted to each other. She was the only daughter of the poet James Matthews. To my way of thinking, you should never start a relationship with your friend's sister, never mind your friend's favourite daughter. But I couldn't help it.

When Terry came to town with her group of friends, doing a countrywide scan of the political and cultural environment among activists and expressing themselves on their take of the way forward, she was irresistible. Among the group was Zo Kota from Gugulethu, while the others were from the Cape Flats and rural areas such as Genadendaal. They raised the ante and brought issues such as gender equality and the abuse and oppression of women by male chauvinists into the debate. They criticised Black Consciousness for being self-righteous. For instance, reckless comrades would refer to 'blue-eyed devils' when referring to whites. Terry's team said that they were also black, but had blue eyes.

Terry and I could not be separated. We would hold hands and steal kisses whenever there was a chance. We had eyes for each other only. It was syrupy sweet walking the dusty streets of Alex with her, lost to the world. They were guests of the Serote family on 16th Avenue. One of my comrades and friends, Eddie Ntlhane, gave up his room for me on 15th Avenue, near the bus rank, so that I could be near her. I was smitten, my hormones in overdrive. I even had a love pimple on my chin.

I would playfully irritate Terry by referring to Cape Town's liberalism. She accused me of being aloof and a snob. My powers of persuasion and box of rhetorical tools were not so strong, then. I was tongue-tied before her pointed analysis. But despite our robust debates, we were lovers still. I liked the challenge because she confronted everything I said. She also questioned my diction. She told me that she and her friends had gone to the Writers' Association of South Africa to question the association's elitism. They must have met with Zwelakhe Sisulu and Phil Mthimkhulu. They emphasised the importance of democracy and consultation with the masses, rather than the leadership adopting a know-it-all approach.

The Writers' Association eventually mutated into the Media Workers' Association of South Africa, to accommodate the workers in printing shops and the broadcasting media. It launched a wage strike in 1981, which resulted in the regime placing banning orders on Joe Thloloe, Phil Mthimkhulu, Mathatha Tsedu, and Zwelakhe Sisulu.

Terry and her crew went back to the Cape peninsula. The saying that absence makes the heart grow fonder did not work for me. After a few long-distance telephone calls, that was it.

13

The Point of No Return

AZAPO pitched up to lead action supporting the rent and services complaints of the Tembisa residents, and a boycott was agreed on. The residents marched out of the meeting and onto the streets to mobilise other community members. In the early hours of the following day, the Special Branch swooped on all known activists. I was picked up at home by my old adversary, van Niekerk, and detained under the General Law Amendment Act. This allowed for fourteen days' detention while the police worked out a charge. The detainee could be held in solitary confinement and was not allowed access to lawyers or a doctor during that time. The fourteen days could be extended indefinitely, until the person was charged or the police decided to release them. This law was a modified version of the Sobukwe Clause, under which Robert Sobukwe was kept in isolation on Robben Island for a year, and in his case this was repeated for nine years.

I was way past the age of innocence this time around. I had read up on the detention laws and educated myself about the few rights I had. I also knew that I had the right to ask for the written regulations.

In that early-hours swoop, many other political activists were detained; mainly the branch members in Tembisa. The AZAPO national leadership was also detained and brought to the Benoni regional offices of the Special Branch. While we were waiting in the charge office with other detainees, George Wauchope, the national administrative secretary, told everyone to stand up, because the president was coming in. Everyone stood up, including the police. In came Kehla Mthembu, president of AZAPO, in handcuffs. The prank broke the tension and we all laughed out loud.

The police had no intelligence about the political fissures in AZAPO, despite the public nature of the leadership squabbles. The former AZAPO president, Curtis Nkondo, had been quietly dismissed from office because he was a confirmed Charterist – a follower of the Freedom Charter. Nkondo had caused a ruckus with his unorthodox Black Consciousness views when he asked the Progressive Federal Party member of parliament Helen Suzman to help have his brother, Zinjiva Winston Nkondo (otherwise known by his guerrilla name of Victor Matlou), released. He had been abducted while on his way to Botswana on a flight that crossed South African territory. This abduction clearly flouted the international law of travel and protection of refugees. Zinjiva was a poet in exile. Pleading for mercy from whites was never done in Africanist and Black Consciousness circles. The leadership of the student wing, the Azanian Students' Organisation, had been won over by the Charterists too. The renegades could not be dismissed soon enough. They worked in defiance of the political leadership. In fact, some of the leading members of AZAPO itself, such as Popo Molefe (who chaired the Soweto region), were leaning towards the philosophies of Nelson Mandela while he was in prison.

I was taken to Kempton Park Police Station for detention. The officers put us two to a cell, and I had David Makgakga for company. Bra Day, as we all knew him, was the president of a local football club and had a personable disposition towards everyone. He was in AZAPO and had been assigned to talk on housing issues in the community. He briefed me about the developments that had led to the call for the rent boycott. Those opposing the boycott were people wanting to serve as councillors and puppets of the township superintendent.

With nothing else to do, we formulated a physical exercise programme, and we thoroughly enjoyed it. Even when the police came to take us for interrogation, we would tell them to wait until we had finished our exercises. Our exercise regime was a 40-minute session in the morning, when we ran on the spot, and in the afternoon we spent another 40 minutes doing muscle-building exercises. Bra Day must have been in his mid-forties then, and he had a pot belly, which was his trademark. Men with conservative ideas believed that a pot belly conferred a certain authority that required respect. Beats me why anyone would think this.

In the evenings we entertained ourselves by singing with the other detainees, and we even had poetry readings. I'm very bad at performance poetry, but the comrades asked me to imitate Ingoapele Madingoane. On stage, he had a conversational section doing call-and-return in his poem 'Black Trial'. He would end the performance with his poem 'Africa My Beginning'. I had been part of the workshop preparing Madingoane's work, as I was known by the artists for my understanding of the cultural theory of resistance and national liberation. I was, quite frankly, useless when it came to performance poetry itself. Yet here I was, entertaining the comrades, bellowing out 'Black Trial'.

'Freedom is the law of nature.'

They would all repeat this after me.

'Justice is the universal order of things.'

'Let he who loves me, come to me.'

Pause.

'Let he who hates me, depart from me.'

Their favourite part was when I said, 'I am because you are. And because you are, I am.' I did not like Madingoane's final line, but I said it anyhow: 'We the cursed are most, we the most are the strong.'

African people are not cursed. They are exploited to the bone and dehumanised so that they do not believe in themselves, and this is why they believe that paradise on Earth is lost. Their hope is for peace and harmony in heaven. Or, in primitive terms, they believe that superior magic potions have been unleashed on them by their own neighbours, through the charlatan muti men, to bring them down. Even learned intellectuals believed in this hogwash.

To my bemusement, I had agreed to take a bath in water mixed with aloes and dark grass products when my mother and her prophetess friend in the neighbourhood had asked me to, after the Freedom Charter case in 1979 was won. It seemed harmless, and I did not want to hurt my mother's feelings. When the prophetess asked that my mother put some woollen bangles on my wrists, waist and ankles, I stormed out of the meeting in fury. I was not cursed and I was not going to play the bad-luck game with them. I was a complete free thinker. I did not follow juju practices.

I had always argued playfully with Ingoapele Madingoane on these issues in our poets' workshops. Mchana, as we called him, devotedly followed the writings of the muti man Credo Mutwa. He was uncritical with respect to this man. Mutwa was a tourist attraction for Europeans who wanted to experience primitive Africa and understand exotic artefacts on display, like calabashes and fanciful beads, before buying them. It was business and a misrepresentation of indigenous African cultures. In political terms, it was cultural nationalism that was devoid of resistance to colonialism.

In the interrogation sessions, the head of the Special Branch could not give any satisfactory answers as to why I had been detained. I did not have a house; I was not even on the waiting list for a house. I did not belong to a civic organisation. I was not even thinking of getting married. I deliberately bombarded him with this ridiculous approach.

My point was, why was I being detained under these circumstances? I was not interested in co-operating with him and his men at all. I told him so to his face, in the presence of one of the black policemen. The police were and are hierarchical, and the higher ranks are deified. I hit him with arguments from unexpected angles. He retorted that the detention laws were made legally in parliament, with the political opposition free to have their say. This was a democratic South Africa, he assured me. Yet here they were making laws among themselves as whites and using them to oppress us, who had never been consulted in the first place. The police used *krag* – force – as a standpoint. They took orders and implemented those orders without questioning, whereas I questioned everything I came across. We were from opposite ends of the spectrum. I asked him to release me or take me back to the cells.

During lunch time, Tlhaki Lekganyane and I were put in a room together, guarded by the two black policemen who had been present during the interrogations. We were given good food, unlike the stuff that was given to criminals. We were left to eat in peace and quiet. We engaged in small talk, but showed respect to our guards as common courtesy.

The one policeman, speaking isiXhosa, could not contain himself. He had been in Tlhaki's interrogation session. He waxed lyrical at the way in which the white policeman had been told off and educated about the conditions of the black man in occupied Azania. Tlhaki always used the SASO rhetoric and posture in politics, when addressing the ills of society. He spoke for the black man. SASO activists used it on their platforms to mobilise the public. The two policemen actually asked us to have as many children as possible. With black men like us, who did not fear the white people in authority and could tell them what the real problem with whiteness was, the struggle would be won very quickly by the next generation. They were really moved.

On day eleven in detention, I was called from my cell in the morning and told that I was being released. James Moleya had also taken a nonco-operative approach, and he was being released too. Previously he had spent a year-long spell in detention without trial under Section 10, and been kept in Modderbee Prison with other national leaders from 19 October 1977 until the end of 1978. The other detainee due for release was a young high school student, Brian Gezani Ndlovu.

Two white policemen drove us home in a sedan. It was good to be released from detention. However, the struggle continued. Aluta continua.

Ravan Press colleague Glenda Webster, in expressing her support for me, had launched a one-person picket at the Kempton Park Police Station, bringing me a bowl of fruit and a change of clothing. She maintained that political detainees had rights too, including that their parents should know about their detention conditions. At the time she was married to David, a senior sociology lecturer at Wits.

I liked that Glenda could explore loopholes in the dastardly laws and demand that innocuous legalities be exercised for detainees, to embarrass and expose the ridiculous nature of the apartheid authorities. Needless to say, I had not received the food parcel or clothing she had brought. The police had helped themselves, I imagined.

The Websters invited me to their house in an abandoned mining town west of Johannesburg. We had lively evening discussions on the culture of resistance. David was well aware of the *ngoma busuku* night shows organised for Denver Hostel folks and northern-suburbs domestic workers in Johannesburg, in contrast to the US-influenced township culture. Groups like Ladysmith Black Mambazo were the main drawcards at these events, although they were not promoted widely and they had no vinyl recordings then.

I could not help but notice the Websters' interesting library of leftist-inclined books. I took notes. These books were readily available in the bookshops. What the Special Branch were doing in harassing black collectors of books was illegal bullying. David went further and introduced me to the classic social realist novels of Émile Zola, Gustave Flaubert, Maxim Gorky, and others. I found a perfect fit with what we in the *Staffrider* editorial collective were aiming to achieve.

Glenda was keen to have me write an autobiography, but she was perhaps somewhat overbearing in this. I had finished three chapters of the draft, when my conscience told me not to do what she wanted. It was not kosher to respond to the whims of others. It was even more difficult because a white person was now beginning to want to control my thoughts. She was condescendingly nasty. I could not allow myself to be a Man Friday created by a colonial settler Robinson Crusoe. I would not sell my mind and soul in exchange for acceptance in to Western civilisation. I liked Glenda as a friend, but did not appreciate being groomed and guided by her. I could make up my own mind about what I wanted to write.

David Webster took supporting detainees to an advanced level. He led the Detainees' Parents Support Committee, an affiliate of the United Democratic Front. The Civil Co-operation Bureau, a government-sponsored death squad, found his exposure of their criminal activities, through helping the tortured detainees, unacceptable, and in 1989 he was shot and killed in front of his new house in Troyeville. By then he had been long divorced from Glenda.

Webster was not the only person murdered in cold blood in front of their house. A similar fate awaited Dr Fabian Ribeiro and his wife Florence, who had treated the victims of police torture and made their findings available internationally.

My fellow detainee, James Moleya, was a mature and go-to veteran politician. The 1976 generation used him as a reference point. He was about ten years older than me. His political network was wide. He was employed as an art director at the advertising company, BBDO. Suzette Mafuna, formerly of *The World*, was a copywriter there too.

After office hours, the three of us would visit and give moral support to the Mandela household, in Orlando West. Zindzi Mandela was in charge while her mother, Winnie, languished in isolation in the backwater dorp of Brandfort in the Orange Free State. Winnie Mandela had assumed the position of national spokesperson of the struggle inside the country. She authoritatively supported the organisations rising up against the regime and gave interviews to the international news agencies. The ban was meant to gag her forever, but she broke it regularly.

Zindzi wrote poetry. On these evenings she and I would compare notes and discuss the other areas of the political struggle. At first she could not understand why I was so attached to the PAC, but we shared a political tolerance and enjoyed the good company.

We had these deep discussions with Moleya, too. To hear them you might have wondered why we tolerated one another. Indeed, Moleya was hoping to persuade me to work for the ANC underground.

Unbeknown to him, I was in a PAC underground network with Tlhaki and Clement Senyatsi, a Putco bus driver. The PAC encouraged their cells to operate as small units, instead of the bigger groups that had been easier for the authorities to crack in the 1960s. Senyatsi was exemplary in his work for the PAC. He even offered to give up his job and do PAC work full-time.

Eventually James Moleya realised I could not be persuaded to join the ANC, despite the torture I had endured and the fact that I had been convicted for possession of the Freedom Charter. I was a PAC man.

Meer had made a plea for the defence and analysed the social background of each one of us. Despite her expert testimony, the prosecutor did his best to undermine her, and he showed her no respect.

On 9 December 1987, the day of sentencing, the Security Branch escorted the kwela-kwela truck carrying the three of us to court. As we had to come from Vereeniging, and as only back roads were used, we arrived at court four hours later than scheduled. Dolly Mokgatle, our attorney, later told me that the state had announced that a rescue mission by armed APLA 'terrorists' to take us to Tanzania had been foiled by the police. She also said the delay was an old prosecutor's trick to anger the magistrate before he announced the sentence.

The gallery was full that day. There were reporters from the *Sowetan*, *City Press*, and the Sunday papers.

Magistrate Hoffman found us all guilty of belonging to a banned organisation and of the terrorism charges. He spoke about me for the better part of his judgment. He said I was an executive committee member of the PAC leadership, that I was responsible for poisoning the minds of the youth, and that I needed to be punished severely because I was not taking advantage of the reforms the government was making with respect to their treatment of black people in the urban areas. Instead I was operating against the government. He accused me of being a propagandist like the Nazi Goebbels, spreading messages to confuse society. He remarked on my intelligence and said that from my testimony it was clear that I was not to be taken lightly. Even though I had not been trained for military activity, he was going to punish me severely, and he cited my previous conviction for possession of banned literature.

He sentenced Khonongwe to eight years for terrorism and two years for belonging to the banned PAC. Cele received the me. He stated that he had only met me a day before our arrest. He also put on the record that he had travelled with an equally senior political leader and APLA high-command member, Castro Rouge, alias David Phillip, to meet up with me. Ntsala explained how my two co-accused, Cele and Khonongwe, had attended commando courses in Libya and specialised in close combat. He had smuggled them into the country in an operation that aimed to raise the image of APLA through the use of Scorpion machine pistols. He had sent six sets of three APLA guerrilla units into the Transvaal. The defence counsel tried to punch holes in his evidence, but he remained steadfast.

While awaiting trial, we were held at Johannesburg Prison, where they also held state-of-emergency detainees. I managed to establish contact with the PAC president, Zephania Lekoane Mothopeng, and he gave Mark Shinners, and at times Jafta Masemola, the responsibility of liaising with us. We wrote extensive political notes and smuggled them to each other. Masemola was innovative and brave, and insisted on having things his way instead of kowtowing to the prison authorities. He made it a point to meet at the dispensary for prisoners, under the pretext that we were both ill.

Shinners told me of the death of my friend and comrade in Atteridgeville, Buti Norman Mnisi. He was killed one night on the streets of Soshanguve, walking home from a political session with PAC underground operatives. The news of his death was a heavy burden, especially in prison where there was no-one to console me or talk to about the tragedy with. I imagined that Mnisi, who was a man of the people, would have fought his assassins.

As the trial drew to a close, the case was transferred to the Springs Magistrates' Court because of an overload of cases. So many people were being charged with so many different misdemeanours that the courts couldn't cope. In our case, Prof Fatima a site of struggle, but this is exactly what I did. In short, I said that I knew what the aims and objectives of the PAC were, and that I sympathised with the organisation. South Africa was under white rule and its policies of apartheid were oppressive to black people. Banned organisations such as the PAC were prohibited from expressing themselves because they stood for the truth. I was not a trained soldier, I told the court, but I understood that the guerrillas were not bandits. They were political fighters. My testimony was that the PAC had legitimacy in the eyes of the African people. I could not denounce a liberation movement that stood for my own emancipation. My attitude was different from Sobukwe and Mothopeng in their trials in 1960 and 1978, in which they refused to plead before a white judiciary.

Mapalakanye and Mfundisi were represented by attorney City Morobe and advocate Modise Khoza. They both refused to plead. In court, Mapalakanye stated that he had been tortured and forced to implicate the accused in his statement to the magistrate. He described how the security police had beaten him on his genitals and kept him in solitary confinement without access to his lawyers for more than eight months. Their refusal to testify meant that the state opened perjury cases against them, but their attorneys managed to get them off – small but motivating victories.

The hearing was not open to the public when I took the stand, or when the two witnesses refused to testify. It was even stricter when Mr X, the state's main witness, Percy Ntsala, was called to give evidence. He described the PAC strategy of a people's war, the build-up by politicising and agitating the masses, and how this first phase was mostly not about engaging in shooting confrontations with the enemy forces. He said he was the field commander responsible for the infiltration of the Azanian People's Liberation Army from Botswana into South Africa. He had been informed that inside the country he would get instructions from kept quiet, and I suppose he was aware of the end goal of freedom for all. My mother-in-law, Ma Mosala, attended the trial and made her presence felt by talking out loud to me in the dock before court started. She was on the board of directors at Skotaville Publishers, along with George Negota, a businessman, former *Pace* magazine editor Mathilda Thokozile Masipa, Advocate Modise Khoza, Sipho Sepamla, Father Buti Tlhagale, James Seutloadi, and others I cannot recall.

Negota, as chairperson of the board, and Mutloatse, as the managing director, played a significant supporting role by offering moral and material assistance to my family during this time. They paid my salary every month. They also arranged for my family to buy township property through the 99-year leasehold. (Africans were not allowed to purchase property or have full property rights in the urban areas.) I will forever be grateful to these two gents for the support they provided me and my family, when they had no obligation to do so.

In preparation for the trial, my comrades had attorney Ray Tucker taken off my case, without consulting me. I assume this was because he was white. Yet Skotaville had a long and warm relationship with him, as he was our company lawyer. In fact he had been responsible for getting the Skotaville vehicle released from the police pound after my arrest. He had also been Sobukwe's attorney. Being in detention, I could not be consulted on these decisions.

The witnesses in the trial were mostly police officers, although one, an interpreter, was called to give evidence regarding Terra Khonongwe's statement (since Terra was illiterate). When I was on the witness stand I made it clear that my statement had been made under duress, while I was being tortured by Captain Badenhorst. The prosecutor hadn't expected us to use the witness stand as

159

court as our trial advocate. Instead, Advocate Bernard Ngoepe acted for us, with senior advocate Louis Skweyiya in the team.

Skweyiya had acted for Andrew Zondo, a guerrilla from uMkhonto we Sizwe who had defied their policy of not placing the lives of civilians in danger by setting off a bomb in Amanzimtoti, near restaurants. There were several casualties in the incident. Zondo was arrested, charged with murder and other lesser charges, found guilty, and sentenced to death. Professor Fatima Meer, a sociologist at the University of Natal, had written up this story and submitted her manuscript to Skotaville, where I had worked with her on the text. Our intention had been to publish it in 1986, as part of a campaign to have the death sentence commuted. Fatima Meer was a mother to us, the younger generation of the struggle. I had also edited her biography of Nelson Mandela, *Higher Than Hope*. I was professional and never objected to her point of view, but made editorial comments and suggestions to enhance the quality of the book.

In addition to our appointed advocates, Advocate Essop Patel, a friend, poet and Ravan Press author, offered his services. Many were the hours he and I had spent discussing literature and protest activities. He had once taken me to his home in Newtown on a Saturday afternoon for samoosas and tea.

On one of her visits, Dikonelo brought me greetings from Don Mattera, who also sent me his recently published autobiography, *Memory is the Weapon*. He had autographed it for the two of us, with the inscription, 'Love Conquers All.' My uncle, Jack Monageng, was a huge presence in court at the Kliptown Magistrates' Court, despite his diminutive figure. He was a bantamweight but a man of stature in Soweto, where he was a coal merchant and had general dealer outlets in various parts of the sprawling township. My family had never taken a negative view of my activities. My mother had not once objected to my political activism. My father trusted so easily nail me on the cross in front of the devil? I could not believe it. Either Mfundisi was letting me know that it was safe, and everyone had fled their safe houses, or he realised that I knew nothing because of my month-long detention. Guerrillas were mobile, on the move all the time, particularly when members of a unit were apprehended by the police. My detention was known and had been reported in the newspapers. It followed that our operatives would have moved to new safe houses. My mind spun as I tried to stay ahead of the police.

I was taken back to Jeppe. In the evening, a four-car convoy returned me to Protea Glen Police Station. Badenhorst and his torture crew were there too, as was Viljoen. I was now to take them to the home of Maropodi Mapalakanye, who also knew about the guerrilla movements. I had no option but to do this, and Mapalakanye was taken into custody. Early in the morning I was driven back to Jeppe Police Station and told that they now had Mapalakanye and four others in detention. The investigating officers now had a field day, confusing all the detainees attached to the PAC case, and brainwashing some of them. They even questioned my pregnant wife, but she told them she had no knowledge of what was going on.

I eventually went to trial on 11 February 1987. I was the first accused, with Njabulo Mandla Cele and Thembinkosi Terra Khonongwe as the second and third accused respectively. The indictment was for engaging in terrorism and belonging to a banned organisation. The charge sheet had 43 witnesses. When we first appeared at the Johannesburg Magistrates' Court, Advocate Dikgang Ernest Moseneke assured us that we would be represented by attorneys from the Black Lawyers Association, with Mojanku Gumbi and Dolly Mokgatle in charge. Because Moseneke was part of the internal PAC leadership, it wasn't prudent to have him in young United Democratic Front-affiliated people detained under state-of-emergency decrees.

When I complained that I had not seen a doctor, the police agreed to let me see the district surgeon and asked me not to talk about the torture. I told the district surgeon I needed to see a magistrate to report the torture. I showed no visible signs of torture, but there was blood on my clothes. The magistrate took a sworn statement from me detailing the torture by Badenhorst and his gang.

I had hoped that by talking to the magistrate I would create a trail of evidence. I had hoped, too, that Percy's declarations would go no further. After a month in detention, I learned that my wife and family had been searching for me in vain. Fortunately, a woman who worked with the female prisoners at Jeppe was able to get word to Dikonelo, who was then able to send in solution for my contact lenses. For a month I had been unable to see properly. Now I was able to read, and as the United Democratic Front comrades had smuggled in newspapers – called *iimpukane* (flies) – I could catch up on what was happening in the country.

Then once again I was taken to Protea Glen Police Station. All they told me was that I was in major trouble. They had Vincent Mfundisi in custody, and he had told them that I was the only one who knew where the APLA guerrillas on the East Rand were housed. Clearly he had not withstood their torture and had talked. I retaliated by saying that I had been in detention for a month and could not possibly know what Mfundisi was talking about. Their next move was to bring in Percy, who disclosed that eighteen guerrillas had been infiltrated from Botswana and had reported to us. I must know where they were.

The inside of my mouth dried up as I tried to evade answering these allegations. My stomach was ice cold. How could people I

Percy. Where had we been in Zeerust? Whose house did we visit? I denied everything. I told them Percy had organised everything. I was just the driver. He was in charge. The only thing I could lose was my life. They used the good cop, bad cop method, but I stuck to my story.

We were next driven to Mafeking to a counterinsurgency army base. Naked except for a grey blanket, and chained with leg irons, I was thrown into a cell and allowed to sleep for the first time. Percy was in the cell next door. There were two uMkhonto we Sizwe guerrillas next to him.

I was kept there for seven days without being asked a single question. Percy, on the other hand, was co-operating with the Boers, phoning comrades in Botswana and luring them to selected spots. He took instructions from the Boers. It was clear to me that this detention centre was an entry point for turncoats, soon to be agents of the enemy.

When we had a chance to talk, I told him that he was wrong to co-operate. He must resist. Guerrillas did not cower and surrender to the enemy. What I said went in one ear and out the other. His wife and child, whom he had not seen since going into exile in 1978, where brought to the centre. I began to realise that his story was unclear. It seemed as if he had already been an informer for the police when he went into exile. He identified the comrades when shown their photographs. He was clearly co-operating fully.

I was next taken to Jeppe Police Station and officially detained under Section 29 of the Internal Security Act. This meant they could keep me in solitary confinement for up to six months before charging me, and then the incarceration could be extended for a further six months. At Jeppe I encountered three other Section 29 detainees who were all unionists. They had been part of the 1986 strike when they were detained. The next batch to arrive were

Somehow they lifted me off the floor. I think there were five of them, with Badenhorst directing operations. I found it difficult to breathe, especially when they started punching my body, hitting me in the face until there was blood in my mouth, on my lips, running from my nose. They twisted my testicles. The pain was searing. I have no idea how long this torture lasted.

Throughout, Badenhorst kept up his questions, although they were not about the arrest. He was playing serious mind games. He wanted to know how old I was. When was my birthday? Did I have children? What did I wish for in my life? Had I been on holiday? All the time the punching continued. He said I'd never see my next birthday. I was 27. The thought of dying by the age of 28 helped me bear the pain. I was not going to give in to my tormentors. I would not allow my enemy to control my mind. I decided that I would win the duel with Badenhorst if I came through the torture without breaking down.

At some stage I felt as if Badenhorst had grabbed my life in his hands, and with one more squeeze I would be gone. He knew it too. He whispered into my ear that I should say my last prayer. I was not going to take final instructions from my enemy, from my killer, come what may. I kept telling myself that these men were cowards. Five against one. I was going to win eventually; the revolution would win. They could do what they wished with my body, but my mind was untouched. I was ready to face my death. I was not afraid.

I don't know how long this torture session lasted. Still blind-folded, in handcuffs, with blood and mucus flowing down my naked body, they walked me to a room with wet floor tiles and hosed me down. The cold water was devilish.

By now I had not slept for three days straight. I was taken back to the interrogation room and given my clothes. Once I was dressed they wanted to know again how I had met up with now handcuffed both Percy and me and called over the security police. It was the evening of 9 September 1986.

We were stripped naked and searched, then taken to the Koster Police Station and separated. I kept my cool, addressing the police in Afrikaans and English. By six the next morning they had realised from their records that I was a PAC leader. They were triumphant.

One of them said to me, 'Okay, Seroke, you are now arrested with your soldier. This means the war is over for you. You are defeated. Stop thinking that you have anything to offer. We can kill you now and say you tried to escape. We can do anything we want with you.'

For the next couple of hours they interrogated me in two-hour stretches with thirty-minute breaks in between. Afterwards I was transferred to Potchefstroom. Here the process continued, first with one officer and then with another. I was kept standing the entire time, and it was only when they stopped for lunch that I was able to sit for a brief twenty minutes. In the evening, I was taken to the Protea Glen Police Station in Soweto for more interrogation.

Here I was kept in a room, naked, handcuffed, and blindfolded. My 'old friend' Viljoen came in with Percy. Despite the blindfold I could see that he was also naked, and covered in blood. Viljoen told me Percy had told them everything, the truth. I thought they were probably playing mind games with me, and putting me under pressure, making me think that Percy had cracked. They had all the details of why we went to Zeerust and what we did there.

'Now tell us the rest of the story and not this rubbish that you've been telling us,' Viljoen said.

I think it was about midnight when another Security Branch officer I know only as Badenhorst and his crew came in. They told me my hour of truth had now come.

153

need to bring in more arms. These contacts had brought in more arms and left them in the village of Gopane, near Zeerust.

I realised I needed to move the equipment to Johannesburg, so I contacted Percy Ntsala, the field commander normally based in Botswana, and we decided to drive to Gopane immediately. We left early the next morning, but as we neared Zeerust the car's accelerator cable snapped. We were ten kilometres from Gopane and the sun had not yet risen. There was nothing for it but to do walk. Our intention was to get a mechanic to fix the car and head back to Johannesburg before dusk.

We got to the village at six and our hosts suggested we sleep while they arranged for a mechanic to repair our car. By two o'clock the car was ready. It then turned out that the cache was in a field at Ramotswa, fifty kilometres away. Once there, an old man helped us recover the weapons, and we returned to the Gopane house. After dinner we were on our way. In Zeerust we stopped at a garage for petrol, and from the local taxi drivers I gathered intelligence about any possible roadblocks. They told us to take the longer Rustenburg route, but Percy was convinced that the Koster route was safer, and I bowed to his judgement. Then just outside Swartruggens we passed a stationary police car, and after that we ran into a roadblock. I was used to roadblocks, so I nonchalantly took out my driving license and complied with the officers searching the car. They looked in the back and then waved us on. For some reason, at this point Percy got out of the car. He had a copy of a PAC booklet in his shirt pocket and the green, black and gold colours caught the attention of a black policeman. He stopped Percy and apprehended him. As I was about to drive away, I, too, was stopped.

The roadblock seemed to be manned by a farm commando, some members of the SA Defence Force and Security Branch. They entry and exit points to the townships and distributed thousands of leaflets promoting their operations.

This APLA unit had acquired its name because they used Škorpion machine pistols that the PAC had received from (then) Czechoslovakia. They were over-enthusiastic and, brandishing Scorpion pistols, had taken funds in broad daylight from a few enterprises in the industrial areas of Wynberg and Bramley. This earned them the name Scorpion Gang, created by the government's Bureau of Information.

Further propaganda by the police was initiated after an open skirmish with trained guerrillas Tshepo Lilele and Neo Khoza in the company of a local cadre, where once again Škorpion machine pistols were used. This happened on Corlett Drive in the white suburb of Bramley, near Alexandra. Tshepo had several safe houses in Tembisa and Soweto to hide in, since he had been operational as a commissar in the Pretoria, Witwatersrand and Vaal area for more than two years when the incident occurred. I had gone with him to Taung and Pampierstad to search for Themba Pikwana, who commanded the APLA operations on the SA Defence Force in Alex and elsewhere. APLA guerrillas were mobile, agile and nimble, as a rule.

The battle of Bramley brought the attention of the police closer to the area where I operated. We learned that some of the fellows in our network had disappeared and then returned, and were acting suspiciously. It was becoming dangerous. The link with the command in Botswana was also suspicious. A courier had disappeared too, while taking an arms cache to Ramotswa.

I received a call from APLA contacts in Soweto, asking for an urgent meeting, and I agreed to meet them in a friend's garage. They had information that the courier with the arms cache had gone over to the enemy. They were aware that I knew where other guerrillas were positioned in the Transvaal and that I would now badly managed by the leadership and the animosity trickled down to the supporters of both groups.

With the financial muscle of Kagiso Trust, the United Democratic Front went from strength to strength, giving a complexion to the struggle that suited the European communities and pandered to white fears of an Africanist-type black domination. Africanism was deliberately associated with the *swart gevaar* monster and Africanists were cast as the ones who wanted to drive whites into the sea.

The United Democratic Front appropriated the word non-racialism, which was first used by the Africanists to mean that the race concept could only be applied to humanity as whole, and instead used it to mean the co-operation of mixed races. The word and its new meaning of multiracialism gained currency. It still meant a united South Africa of four main races, namely the whites, the Indians, the coloureds, and the black Africans.

The PAC's strategy was to increase the fighting capacity of the Azanian masses, to a conduct people's war against the military powerhouse of South Africa. APLA believed in carrying out the fight at a mortal level. The guerrillas were trained to engage the enemy at close quarters, and did not discount the sabotage of economic installations. The Boers would easily be demoralised when they had to take body bags to the families of their soldiers.

Patrick Laurence, a senior political correspondent for *The Star* newspaper, wrote that the PAC's guerrilla warfare strategy, with its chilling 'One Settler, One Bullet' slogan, put fear into white communities.

At the same time, an APLA unit in Alexandra gained notoriety in the media as the Scorpion Gang. It attacked the police and the army in 1985. The unit waged a six-day war with the police in the township after mourners had been attacked at the night vigil of an activist. They attacked soldiers on sentry duty at strategic

16

The Arrest in Koster

Guerrilla warfare uses lethal means. It is about conducting a just war as a means to an end. In the Pan Africanist Congress of Azania, it was a continuation of the political struggle for land and dignity. A guerrilla was a political fighter.

The Poqo insurrection between 1961 and 1967 had been used by the apartheid authorities to propagate the idea of the *swart gevaar* threat as a danger to white domination. This threat had to be suppressed by any means. *Swart gevaar* was often used to manipulate voters in the whites-only elections. It became the sum total of what were understood to be 'white fears'.

With the rise of the United Democratic Front, the strategy was to unite the ethnic, tribal and racial entities against monstrous and divisive apartheid projects such as the Tricameral Parliament and the homelands. The slogan was 'Apartheid Divides, UDF Unites'. It caught on like wildfire.

The secretary-general of the South African Council of Churches, Bishop Tutu, hosted a high-powered visit by the US senator Edward Kennedy, who came on a fact-finding mission. The senator brought an international news crew with him and talked to everyone in the conflict, from PW Botha to big-name personalities such as Rev Allan Boesak, Dr Nthato Motlana, and others.

The new national organiser for AZAPO, Thabo Sehume, now unbanned, staged a 'Yankee, go home' protest against Kennedy's visit. It irritated many, who saw it as obstructionist. The United Democratic Front condemned AZAPO openly. The clash was

arrests and trials of the commanders of APLA, namely Jan Shoba and his four co-accused, and Enoch Zulu, Achmad Cassiem, and others. Other fronts opened in the churches, in journalism and in business forums.

The PAC underground was fast reaching the critical mass that would enable the organisation to set up a political front and articulate the position of the liberation movement in overt ways.

In the midst of all this positive growth, I met Dikonelo Mosala, who had joined the typesetting team at Skotaville. Work was mounting up, with almost twenty titles being published each year. We were even buying rights to books such as *Where There is No Doctor* and translating them into several local languages.

For both of us it was love at first sight. The problem was that she was a friend's daughter. Ma Mosala was a director of the family division of the South African Council of Churches and an English drama teacher and short-story writer. She'd resigned from teaching Bantu Education in 1976. We had become friends, and now I had fallen for her last-born daughter. This was the second time my love life had been so complicated. What was I getting myself into, I wondered?

It wasn't long before Dikonelo and I had established a love nest in one of the boutique hotels in Braamfontein. I introduced her to my parents, and the family welcomed her. I then sent a delegation to ask for her hand in marriage, in the traditional way. My uncle Jack Monageng, in Orlando East, organised his sons Fistos, Tier and Frans to take part. Mpho and Jacob Sunki Seroke, the other side of the family, from Bethanie, were also part of the delegation. We included the clan in its entirety.

I now had an answer to the question of whether revolutionaries should marry. Sobukwe and others before me had answered in the affirmative, and as all revolutionaries must face the same challenges, why should I be different?

the real deal and we hoped that he would influence Mndaweni to swing the whole of the federation to the Africanists. This strategy pandered to the individuals of influence rather than the rank and file, but we were in a hurry to shore up our position.

Maropodi and I worked on the Johannesburg National African Federated Chamber of Commerce and Industry leader, William McBain-Charles. He was a quick thinker and let us use his car dealership in Doornfontein for our transport needs. He even paid Mafube a performance fee for reading poetry at the chamber's conferences. In turn, Mafube used the labour-union gatherings to recruit members for the PAC. We were also able to mobilise shop stewards in various other unions. For example, Mopholosi Morokong joined the South African Chemical Workers Union and allowed us to infiltrate our Africanists into the union. We also had the support of Mudini, the regional secretary of the Media Workers' Association of South Africa and a journalist for *The Star*, as well as that of Mike Tissong, who was against Black Consciousness but never stood in the way of our operations once they'd been explained to him. Tissong helped me exchange US dollars into rands when I urgently needed cash to fund the transport of APLA guerrillas. He asked no questions and we kept our arrangement on a need-to-know basis. The Media Workers' Association employed Stakes Khala, who had completed his jail sentence for PAC activities. Stakes was a revolutionary African nationalist cast in the mould of Zephania Mothopeng.

The Azanian Youth Unity was gaining ground. Its new members often wanted to be linked with APLA activities, but we were careful to fully assess them first to ensure there would be no security breaches. With the activities of other units in the Orange Free State, Natal, and the Cape Province also growing, the PAC underground was getting attention in the press. There were major was hostile to the PAC, given that the military had taken over the government after a coup. We reckoned that it would be to our advantage to work there, simply because no-one would expect us to operate in such a high-risk environment. Not only did we manage, but we managed well, despite the odds. The entire Transvaal became our happy hunting ground as we recruited young people from the rural areas of Gazankulu, Lebowa, Bophuthatswana, and Venda. We were less successful with Kwa Ndebele, which was riven with internal power politics, while Ka Ngwane was in the ANC's pocket.

The APLA high command were happy with these developments, and they played their role in getting our people to Dar es Salaam. In addition to Tanzania, Siyaya Nkonyeni, who was responsible for training, had agreements with General Mengistu Mariam of Ethiopia to train recruits. The PAC was making diplomatic friends and growing its solidarity and support base. The jokes about our having only fourteen soldiers and a fax machine began to disappear.

In labour, we in the Mafube Arts Commune formed a strategy to bring the Council of Unions of South Africa into the Azanian Confederation of Trade Unions, which would provide a solid support base for the Africanists. We needed a mass-based organisation, rather than an elitist group of intellectuals.

James Mndaweni and Narius Moloto were influential cogs in the decision-making processes of the Council of Unions of SA. We had access to Moloto, a timid character with an affinity for the popular struggles of the masses, although he was also a tribalist and an egotist. Moloto lived in Tembisa, and even though we heard him waxing lyrical about the United Democratic Front, we managed to recruit him. Zakade and Baker Phasha worked on Moloto to politicise him, and afterwards Baker left the country for military training with APLA. Moloto realised that we were my name. This caused the thugs to attack me with knobkerries and stones, and I fell down under the blows to my head and face. Fortunately I was not knocked unconscious and was able to escape. I was bleeding badly by the time I got home, and needed to be admitted to Tembisa Hospital.

The thugs were a gang called the Ninjas. Other political activists had also been attacked in the dark by unknown thugs; in fact, Brian Mazibuko, a June 16 activist and former Robben Island prisoner, was killed in this way in Tembisa.

My encounter with the gangsters was written up in *The Star* by Thembeka Mbobo, who was also an executive member of the African Writers Association. A few days later, while recuperating from my injuries at home, I learned that Chairman John Nyathi Pokela had died at Parirenyatwa Hospital in Harare. It was a devastating blow. It meant that we had to increase the momentum of the PAC's underground work.

A state of emergency had been declared, with the uprisings in the townships in full swing. The youth wanted to play a role in the armed struggle, and the workers wanted to be associated with the PAC. The Azanian Youth Unity seemed to be the best bet to recruit young people – both young men and women – and educate them about the PAC. We could add them to the groups we were regularly sending out of the country.

As part of this rejuvenation process, Vincent Mfundisi and Mudini Maivha, journalists for SABC television and *The Star* respectively, asked to be included in the underground network. I already knew them as PAC operatives and they proposed we run a recruitment campaign to swell the ranks of APLA. We set up a route to Lesotho and let the recruited groups grow organically. After six months, we were sending three intakes a month. From Lesotho, they were taken to Tanzania as refugees seeking educational opportunities. We managed this even though Lesotho respect and co-operation. We understood that Sabelo Phama had good relationships with Chris Hani, Joe Modise, and the rest of the leaders in the ANC's armed wing.

Chairman Pokela agreed with our political views about a socialist Azania. His overriding point was that we could not establish what we envisaged without first resolving the national question. The Africanist view was that the recovery of the land from the possession of the tiny minority of colonial settlers was the strategic goal of the African revolution. The self-determination of the African people was a quintessential requirement for development. It would unlock democracy with a socialist tendency. Without this strategy, he felt we lacked focus and were dangerously playing into the hands of the Charterists.

Undoubtedly, the PAC was muted by the influence of other organisations, such as the Azanian People's Organisation. We weren't articulating the PAC position of leading the people of Azania on the revolutionary path against settler-colonialism, racial and bureaucratic capitalism, and imperialism.

The meeting then redeployed me to do diplomatic work to bring the PAC's political programme to life. My first priority was to raise funds for structures fronting for the PAC, and here I analysed the workings of the Kagiso Trust, which was controlled by Beyers Naudé and the European Economic Community. Most of the funds were going to the Charterists, with the funders influencing how the money was used. I thought it better for the PAC to source funding in the Third World. As a start, I smuggled home about $50 000 from Botswana.

I got back safely, but that night, while watching a movie at my local cinema, I realised I was tense and nervous. I left at the interval and walked home through a dark Tembisa. On the way, I encountered a group of thugs in balaclavas dragging a local girl along the road. She cried for help and called out to me by the enemy soldiers shot him outside the house where he lived. As I understand it, Mnyele worked on his art at night. He must have heard the invaders and tried to escape, but was gunned down. Unbelievably, the raiders stole some of his artworks. I headed to Gaborone for his funeral and also to attend the PAC meeting.

The airport was teeming with Botswana's undercover secret service operatives. They singled me out for questioning and I told them I was travelling alone to spend the weekend there as a tourist. They saw through my fabrications and held me for four hours, until I asked to see their superior. When he arrived, I told him that I was a PAC operative and that he could contact the chief representative, Mzothane, to verify my story. In 30 minutes, Mzothane came to pick me up.

I realised that the Boers would know I was in Botswana, because these officials were spying for South Africa's various secret agencies. It was also possible that the Boers were at the airport and had identified me on the spot.

I was in Gaborone with Mzothane's deputy, Letlapa Mphahlele. We'd arrived the day before the planned PAC meeting. Both men knew the extent of my underground work. The meeting was scheduled to take two hours, but in the end it lasted five. During that time we reviewed the PAC's renewal programme and summed up our experiences. The control of the PAC was completely internal, and one of our major topics was how to infiltrate our fighting forces back into the country. On top of that, we needed a guerrilla-warfare strategy and to determine the role of commissars in preparing the political environment. Victor Sabelo Phama was now our secretary for defence. He had come to the meeting with some leaders from the Azanian People's Liberation Army, and he introduced them to us after the meeting, saying they were able to help with our strategy. Despite the rivalry, APLA and MK worked together on the ground, and there was mutual

Mafatshe, Pitika Ntuli, and Bikka Maseko, who were in exile and isolated from the headquarters in Dar es Salaam.

It so happened that I was in London at the time for a meeting of the African Books Collective. Skotaville was a founder member of the collective, which was administrated by Hans Zell Incorporated. As I was in the city, I was asked to attend the PAC brainstorming session. We discussed the causes and effects of the exile conditions, the problems in the leadership (especially during Leballo's time) and how they could be corrected. It was hoped that the intensifying struggle inside the country would help the PAC reinvent itself.

Chairman Pokela had taught with Sobukwe and was instrumental in the formation of Poqo and its insurrection programme, until he was abducted by apartheid forces in 1967 in Maseru. While imprisoned on Robben Island he led hunger strikes and focused on political education. He also accorded intergenerational unity of the South African Students' Organisation and Black People's Convention leadership with that of the PAC. I particularly admired his desire for education. Despite having two university degrees and extensive teaching experience, he took lessons in accounting. His return to political life was heralded as an indication that the PAC would be renewing itself.

To this end, in June 1985, he organised to meet with the internal underground leadership in Gaborone. Plane tickets were arranged for me and Carter Seleka to attend this high-powered secret meeting. Seleka represented the overt Azanian Youth Unity, while I was brought in because of my underground work in the preparations for the armed struggle.

At that time, Botswana was on high alert. There had been raids by the South African Defence Force and people had been killed. My friend and comrade Thami Mnyele was among those killed;

in the United Nations' special committee against racism, using the platform to champion the 1976 uprisings and liaise with the struggle organisations inside the country. He and Make were struggle icons in the eyes of the Africans in the diaspora. They shared the view of the youth that the armed struggle should be intensified and that diplomatic pressure, such as comprehensive sanctions against South Africa, should be applied. In early 1979, they declared on behalf of the PAC that the 1980s would be the decade of the revolution.

Soon after the triumvirate took charge, there were rumours orchestrated by sinister forces that they were misappropriating funds meant for the military camps. The rival ANC and their backers saw the rumours as an opportunity to campaign against the PAC and declare it ineffective.

When John Pokela and Johnson Phillip Mlambo were released from Robben Island after lengthy sentences, Make stepped down from his position as chairman of the central committee in favour of these two men.

In an in-depth analysis of the PAC in exile by Henry Isaacs, focusing on the internal power struggles in the leadership, his publishers in London (ZED) asked for a co-publishing agreement with Skotaville. When the manuscript needed to be checked for possible libel, we found that it was a scathing attack on the PAC by a subjective writer who let his bitterness overtake the facts. There were others who criticised the PAC's excesses and wrongdoing but were not doing so with an agenda to destroy the liberation movement. Skotaville declined to publish the book.

At this time, a meeting took place in London (organised by Bishop Stanley Mmutlanyane Mogoba, who hosted the meeting in his hotel suite) to revive the internal PAC overt structures and keep the flag flying. Among those at the meeting were Saki

15

The PAC Underground Expands

On the diplomatic front, the Pan Africanist Congress of Azania had been put under heavy pressure to fold up and die. The Organisation of African Unity's liberation committee, under Hashim Mbita's leadership, was cynically making known the internal squabbles of the PAC known, as if they were a permanent feature that could not be resolved. Instead of helping to end the disputes, the liberation committee fuelled tensions by advising the OAU that there were no guerrillas in the camps. Mbita was under the influence of the African National Congress, which was calling for the expulsion of the PAC from the OAU and for it to no longer be recognised as a liberation movement. The ANC was campaigning to be the sole representative of the people of South Africa.

After a failed conference in Arusha in 1978 and skirmishes in the military camps in Tanzania, in which David Sibeko was killed, the PAC was rudderless. In Dar es Salaam, another leader, Vusi Linda Make, had miraculously survived an assassination attempt by hiding in a cupboard when assassins entered his apartment and shot randomly. Mbita and his cohorts took advantage of these events and capitalised on the PAC's disarray.

Prior to the conference and the assassinations, Sibeko, Make and Elias Ntloedibe had been charged with the leadership after President PK Leballo had been forced to resign. There were extraneous destabilising forces at play, and there were grievances about the running of the PAC by this triumvirate. This put enormous pressure on the three men. Sibeko had been a catalyst

139

The Special Branch could not pin me down, but they made it clear that they knew what I was doing for the PAC. We had restructured the cell as the political work expanded, but kept matters on a need-to-know basis.

The Congress of South African Trade Unions was also formed, to express the needs of trade unions in place of the defunct South African Congress of Trade Unions, an arm of the equally defunct Congress Alliance. COSATU not only fulfilled a role in labour relations, but also worked with the ANC, as had its predecessor.

Although the country was entering a time of increasing political turbulence, the Freedom Charter was unbanned in 1985. Meanwhile, repression happened everywhere, with the police enforcing dreadful conditions in the townships.

The PAC was regrouping, and its recruits were highly politicised under the motto serve, suffer and sacrifice. We had whites in our ranks, including visiting communists from the Benelux countries, and none of our recruits questioned their presence. We were transparent and clear, explaining the need for our own Africanist organisations, to add to the work of the Azanian Youth Unity.

The Mafube Arts Commune was formed to fulfil this purpose. It was easier to mobilise with poetry than with long and convoluted speeches. With Maropodi Mapalakanye, Jerry Mpe Figlan, and Zakade and Mopholosi Morokong, we used our knowledge in the arts to form a core that believed in a people's art of resistance.

Also in 1983, the PAC chief representative in Botswana, Chris Maseko, defected to the South African Police, where his father worked as a policeman. When the PAC had deployed him to Gaborone from Tanzania, his family had used the contact with him to poison his mind and convince him to join a network of askaris and informers. Tlhaki and I had worked closely with him, completely unaware that he was taking our reports to the upper echelons of the military. Maseko's betrayal put our underground work at great risk. Nevertheless, the leadership of the mission in exile was growing stronger under the authority of John Nyathi Pokela, who had been in prison for thirteen years from 1968.

the international book fair in Frankfurt and the International Book Fair of Radical Black and Third World Books, organised by John La Rose, in London. In southern Africa, the Zimbabwe International Book Fair was a great attraction.

I used these opportunities to travel as a cover to do PAC work. I interacted with most of the leaders. Mike Ngila Muendane was the secretary for labour. He assisted in connecting the above-ground activities on the labour front with PAC-supporting solidarity groups in Europe. The purveyors of Marxism-Leninism and Mao Zedong Thought in Belgium sent their labour unit to South Africa. We had them interact with the labour-union leaders in workshops at Wilgespruit Fellowship Centre in Roodepoort. Reverend Dale White, who ran the centre, was well disposed to wards the PAC.

As part of our contribution to the unity project with the Black Consciousness organisations, the PAC supported the National Forum Conference held at Hammanskraal in 1983. I was assigned a role in the arts and culture section, led by Benjy Francis and Zakes Mofokeng, and I chaired the evening programme, which featured play and poetry readings. I also published the conference papers with funding from the exiled PAC. The National Forum was convened by Saths Cooper, who was a leader of the Azanian People's Organisation. He had been one of the accused during the lengthy trial involving the Black People's Convention and the South African Students' Organisation, which led to his imprisonment on Robben Island for many years.

In 1983, a year after we established Skotaville, the United Democratic Front was established. They used the model of a broad front of civil-society organisations that were against the apartheid authorities. They had funding from the European Economic Community and were definitely a front for the ANC.

135

Churches secretary-general, Rev Frank Chikane. We worked on this document while they were both on the run from the Security Branch and from possible detention under the emergency laws. We also published a collection of essays edited by Charles Villa-Vicencio, which showed that we were not isolated from the broader struggle literature. My PAC work helped, rather than hindered, the spread of ideas as a challenge to the apartheid authorities.

There were interesting sideshows too. When it was clear that Bra Don would not be banned again, we were invited to art gatherings with him. One was at Nadine Gordimer's Parkview house. There must have almost 30 leaders of the arts invited to talk to Hungarian billionaire and patron of the arts, George Soros. Everyone made a case for him supporting their art institution.

Don also took the opportunity to speak, and he criticised the mostly white and liberal participants for being hypocrites. He also spoke directly to Soros: 'You have brought us sorrow, Mr Soros. We are all trying to outshine each other to get access to your money. I thank the host for calling the meeting, but I will not bow to this shame.' I followed behind him as he walked out.

The African Writers Association also held writers' workshops for beginners, and published the lecture notes of Es'kia Mphahlele on drama, fiction and poetry. Novelist Njabulo Ndebele mentored short-story writers at writing clinics we held at Wits University. We also had an extension programme with the National University of Lesotho, where a team went to interact with the likes of Zakes Mda and Sipho Sepamla. During this period I edited several issues of *New Classic*, a literary magazine first published as *The Classic* by 1950s *Drum* writer Nat Nakasa. Sepamla had reintroduced it as *New Classic* in the 1970s, and the African Writers Association published it in the 1980s.

Skotaville published on topical issues, starting with black theologians, political philosophies, and history. We also attended

Skota. He'd been an advocate of African nationalism, and while secretary-general of the South African Native National Congress in 1933, had insisted on the name change to African National Congress. As a chronicler of events, he published *The African Yearly Register*.

One of the first titles we produced was Don Mattera's *Azanian Love Song*, a collection of poetry. His banning order was about to end, and we planned to publish it on the day it expired. He agreed to this, and readily gave me his collection. Fikile Magadlela worked on the artwork for the cover design. Bra Don, as we fondly called him, was good to me. He introduced me to Wednesday-only movies in Fordsburg, where they showed art-house movies. I came to learn all the elements of fiction and literary devices, such as allegory, flashbacks, cameo appearances, powerful diction, and dramatic performance. We would analyse all such issues while we watched these artistic feature films.

The publication of *Azanian Love Songs* was a great success, and as our first book did exceptionally well. The initial print run of three thousand copies quickly sold out, and we had to reprint.

We also published a collection of speeches and sermons, *Hope and Suffering*, by Bishop Desmond Tutu. At the time he was the dynamic secretary-general of the South African Council of Churches. This was by far the best publication, in terms of sales, that Skotaville produced. Altogether, the reprints must have totalled fifteen thousand copies. We also sold translation rights to many countries, which put Skotaville on the map.

There were other notable books, too. For example, we published a book on the social history of the Kagiso Trust by Eric Molobi, who was an executive member of the United Democratic Front. I also procured manuscripts from Catholic liberation theologists, such as Father Albert Nolan, who co-ordinated the production of the Kairos Document with the new South African Council of babies. He had truly lived dangerously, even using his work vehicle to travel to Gaborone and Maseru.

I was susceptible to falling in love with beautiful, innocent girls who had an honest goal to have children and form a stable family. How would I fit in with those dreams? I was an activist for political change. Dangerous. I was in the underground. Very dangerous. I had voluntarily taken on these commitments.

I was attracted to a pretty high school girl with freckles and a disarming smile who lived in the neighbourhood – Stokwana Kekana. I was chivalrous and walked her to the stores when she needed to shop. I made small talk with her to make her feel protected and safe. The ghetto had its two-legged beasts who forced themselves into the skirts of beautiful girls, jeopardising their education with teenage pregnancy and leaving them on the shelf afterwards. I was going to take it step by step with her. After a few days I mentioned that in the fairy tale *Beauty and the Beast*, Beauty grows fond of the Beast because he was caring and friendly. Eventually she falls in love with the Beast and he becomes a fine young man. A prince of peace. I would like to think that she grasped the message in my version of the story, because we were soon an 'item'. I serenaded her with poetry and my own dizzy philosophies of life.

Stokwana lived with her brother at his house. He did his best to keep us apart, by rebuking her when I took her back home after an outing. Tragically, though, he committed suicide, leaving a wife and children. No-one seemed to know what had been troubling him. While Stokwana dealt with this emotional trauma, the struggle sucked me in. Our relationship petered out.

I was then at a new publishing house, Skotaville Publishers, in its editorial section. The African Writers Association had taken a resolution to start a black-owned publishing house. Mothobi suggested the name Skotaville Publishers, after Mweli Trevor

14

Serve, Suffer and Sacrifice

I was now living dangerously. As a sworn enemy of the apartheid and settler state, I could be taken out in the 'total onslaught' battle that President PW Botha was conducting. It went without saying that the liberation movements in exile and at home were heavily infiltrated by enemy agents. I was a nobody. I could be whisked away in a flash and nobody would notice that a nobody was no more. You did not have to be important to feel vulnerable to elimination.

The possibility of arrest and a long time in prison was now very real. Being recalled by the mission in exile of the Pan Africanist Congress of Azania was also possible, as was being abducted by the progressive forces for my own good. It had happened in Zimbabwe, where a prominent journalist in the struggle for Zimbabwe was taken against his will by Zimbabwe African National Liberation Army guerrillas from his ranch while he visited his family. The intention was to protect him from imminent arrest by the Rhodesian security forces.

My sixth sense told me repeatedly that I would be gone (detained or dead) by the year 1988. It was a feeling I couldn't shake, but I told no-one about my fears. They would've said I was crazy to make such predictions about my own life. But I trusted my instincts. In analysing what had happened to me, I found that I did well in odd-numbered years and badly in even-numbered years.

Compared with Tlhaki I was a free man, without a wife and

same sentence. He sentenced me to ten years plus two years for belonging to the banned PAC, which would run concurrently with the sentence for terrorism.

Most of the women – my sisters, cousins, and their friends – in the court behind us cried at the harshness of the sentences, as did our advocate Mokgatle. Without a doubt, he was making an example of us. An appeal was immediately lodged and as the court orderly took us downstairs, Sipho Sepamla called out that we should not worry too much, as the apartheid regime would also be going down very soon.

All I can remember is that there was a long underground tunnel linking the court to the police station. It seemed like a depressingly long walk as we began our prison terms.

17

Robben Island Maximum Security Prison

After the trial I was incarcerated in Johannesburg Prison, which was known as 'Sun City', and my first visitor was Dikonelo. While I had accepted my fate, that my next ten years would be spent behind bars, she had not. We were awkward with one another to begin with, and I made small talk about the baby and the rest of her family members. Then she struck out quick and fast. She told me she was not impressed with my new status as a hero of the struggle. Nor was she going to spend ten long years waiting for me to be released. I listened without interrupting, my mouth dry, a hollowness in my stomach. Before I could say anything, the visiting time was up and, bereft, I watched her walk away.

As I went back to the isolation cell, I felt dizzy and sad. I should have responded to Dikonelo. She was within her rights to feel hurt and resentful that I had not disclosed my political life to her. My life with her had held a secret. And now we had a child – a daughter – Tsholofelo. Hope. Dikonelo's mother, Ma Mosala, wrote me a note to say that hope springs eternal. I read it repeatedly on the days when depression set in. Hope springs eternal.

I wrote Dikonelo a nasty letter. I released her from the traditional marriage and the love relationship with me. She was now 23, with her future before her. I told her I would not hold it against her, she needed to attend to her dreams and wishes, and not tag along by my side. Mine was a rough existence, dry and without romance. As a Category D prisoner I could receive and send a letter only every 60 days, and this was the first letter I sent.

Dikonelo's visit had occurred before Christmas 1987, and it was not until January the next year that I received other visitors. My sister and niece came with wishes and news from the family. My nephew Mike had skipped the country during my trial and was safe in Tanzania with the PAC. My sister's visit was uplifting, and I conveyed her news to my fellow prisoners, especially about Mike being with the PAC. It meant that the struggle was continuing.

We had established a political prisoners' community in Sun City that included the guerrillas from uMkhonto we Sizwe and the activists involved in the Alex uprising in 1986. Among them was a schoolfriend, Obed Bapela, who'd become involved in the ANC's operations. We enjoyed a cordial relationship, despite our different political affiliations. We were mostly trained guerrillas in the group, and we were joined by others sentenced in the northern Transvaal courts. Although we were initially held at Sun City, our ultimate destination was Robben Island.

The Robben Island prison was used by the settler colonialists to put a fear of jail into activists. It was a place away from society. Out of reach and out of mind. In my childhood days I imagined the island as a small place surrounded by a tempestuous sea with inclement weather. The story of Robinson Crusoe and Man Friday, two people on an island, cemented the image of isolation. As my political awareness developed, I read as much as I could about Robben Island and dispensed with the myth.

Among the books I had read was DM Zwelonke's *Robben Island*, and I had met several activists who had returned from spells on Robben Island. Among them was Kaborane Sedibe, who was in the SASO/BPC trial and lived three streets away from me in Tembisa. I had spent a great deal of time organising the revival of the PAC underground with Michael Sthembele Khala, an eloquent storyteller with strong powers of description, who had also served time on the island. Another comrade, Vusi Nkumane, had made a saxophone from scratch while imprisoned on Robben Island. He was a cultural activist and lived in Tembisa. I had read detailed descriptions by those imprisoned on the island in the 1960s, such as Moses Dhlamini's *Robben Island, Hell-Hole: Reminiscences of a Political Prisoner in South Africa*.

Kwame Nkrumah used the term 'prison graduates' for anti-colonialist political activists who were kept in captivity during the struggle. PW Botha had said that South Africa did not have political prisoners, and that those on Robben Island were 'security prisoners'. Yes, but what they called us was neither here nor there. The international community regarded us as political prisoners, and so did the Azanian masses.

In the history books written by Westerners, Bartholomew Diaz, a Portuguese sailor exploring the sea route to the East, fortuitously anchored his ship in Table Bay in 1488, after a hard-hitting 'Cape of Storms' experience. He then sent one of his captains, João Infante, in a small boat across the bay to the island to capture penguins and seals. Historians also have a theory that the island was first 'discovered' by the Phoenicians over 2 000 years ago, and that they found 'traces of Bantu and Khoisan paintings'. Vasco da Gama followed in 1497, and renamed the stormy peninsula the Cape of Good Hope and after escaping to the island when they had met with hostile 'cannibals' on the mainland. It was subsequently used as a dumping ground for prisoners brought from England. Once the Dutch had established a town at the Cape, it was used as a place for mentally ill patients, lepers, and lawbreakers.

(As an aside, Skotaville published the story of Makhanda, the left-handed warrior leader who was banished to Robben Island

and attempted to escape to the mainland, but his boat capsized in the treacherous seas and he drowned. He is also called 'Ukuza kukaNxele', which means the left-handed general who will never land.)

By the time Dikonelo came for her second visit, her parents seemed to have knocked some sense into her. Now she was reconciliatory and understanding of our position. Although my sentence was lengthy, it was not permanent. She had plans to study abroad and keep herself busy. Baby Tsholofelo would be taken care of by the extended family. I could not influence her decisions from prison, and I worried that they would easily forget who I was.

In the winter of 1988, we were taken to Robben Island. The trip was done in stages in a kwela-kwela, with armed police accompanying us in escort vehicles. The first stop was Groenpunt Prison in Bloemfontein. There were other stops to collect prisoners, and when we finally reached Cape Town Harbour we numbered more than 30 political prisoners.

The *Susan Kruger* ferry was our transport to the island. We were locked in a communal cell in the hold and many of us were seasick during the crossing. We reached the island at dusk. Common-law prisoners were at work at the harbour, packing goods under the supervision of the white warders. The weather was cold and it had rained during the day. We were lined up in a column of twos and I was at the tail end of the row with Walk Tall, an MK cadre who had been shot in the leg by police while trying to escape from custody. He had an orthopaedic shoe and limped along to the prison reception, about 400 metres away.

I became prisoner number 51/88. I did not bother to correct the incorrect spelling of my names: they had me as Jackie Steve Seroke. I was given a set of blankets, prison clothing, socks and shoes, a towel, toothpaste and toothbrush, and a set of pyjamas. We were taken to the A Section of the single cells. In each cell was a night-soil bucket, a spring bed and mattress, and a loudspeaker on the wall for announcements and radio broadcasts. The news reader on Radio South Africa kept saying, 'Warning, there is an east-bound, gale-force wind.' The walls of the cell were as cold as ice. Such was my first night in Robben Island Maximum Security Prison.

The warders came in at five the next morning to count us. This was a morning and evening routine. After the morning count we had breakfast in the kitchen and were locked up again. Around eleven there was lunch, and we were allowed to exercise in the yard. I was getting myself ready when Tokyo Sexwale came in and introduced himself and said he was welcoming the ANC cadres. I told him my name and that I was PAC. He welcomed me nonetheless, and then held a meeting with his ANC comrades.

I knew of Sexwale and his co-accused from the news of their trial, which had been held in Pretoria at the Old Synagogue in 1977. The *Sunday Times Extra*, a black supplement, had profiled him as one of the youngest in the trial, and he had been pictured wearing a jumpsuit and saying that he was a karate enthusiast who had married his girlfriend from Swaziland while on trial. His father was a Second World War veteran who lived in Dube, Soweto, in a street that was exclusively for soldiers.

Soon Jan Shoba, a member of the APLA high command who had been arrested with others in 1985, came in to welcome the PAC group. He was responsible for cleaning the kitchen and toilets with disinfectants, and this gave him the opportunity to communicate with PAC people in all the sections. He explained that all political factions lived side by side. Shoba was also able to smuggle in newspapers and information.

In the A Section we had a catering committee, a cleaning group, and a recreation team, in which I participated. The recreation group organised videos once a month, memorial sessions to commemorate dates such as 16 June, and we had a variety of record albums. I joined Vusi Nene's gruelling gym sessions in the mornings. I began to enjoy the communal environment, and when the prison authorities came for interviews, I feigned illness and said that I needed to be in a communal section because I had spent the past three years in isolation.

In August on a Sunday, Tyson Sillah, serving eighteen years, managed to smuggle me out of the A Section, between breakfast and lunch, to his communal cell in G Section, where a birthday celebration for Paul Langa was being held. It was a serious ceremony, with speaker after speaker telling how they knew and appreciated Langa's relationship with the community over the years. His story had also been in the news in the aftermath of the 1976 uprisings in Soweto. He had placed dynamite on the railway line and bombed parts of it. He was soon arrested and eventually sentenced to over eighteen years in prison. Tyson also spoke, and he told of Langa's nickname, Mabujwa, given to him because he always talked about the national bourgeoisie as the sworn enemies of the proletarian revolution.

The PAC leadership in B Section asked me for an article on trade unions and the party's involvement with them. I wrote a 1 500-word analysis of the 1979 Wiehann Commission recommendations and proposals, the legalisation of the trade unions, the response of big business to labour issues, the association with historical union federations such as the South African Council of Trade Unions and the Federation of Free African Trade Unions of South Africa, the 1973 Durban strikes, the consultation process that led to the formation of COSATU, and marginal federations such as the Azanian Confederation of Trade Unions and the Council of Unions of South Africa. I also made various points about the labour-versus-capital discussion from a Marxist point of view.

PEN International encouraged letters and communications with writers in prison. I received more letters from writers than I did from my wife. She just could not write anything more than a paragraph. Eventually she got a bursary to study hotel management and catering at an organisation in Bournemouth, UK. When we were dating I had taken her to posh restaurants in Johannesburg, and she'd noticed my liking for the finer things in life. Her motivation for doing this course was to learn enough so that she could look after her new family, she told me.

While she was in England I arranged for her to see people at the PEN office in London, and to talk to Vusi Nomadolo, who had been the chief representative of the PAC in the UK. Unfortunately, she never told me how these meetings went, and I later learned that her Zimbabwean roommate had completed her letters to me. She was irritated with me for calling her an 'ugly duckling' when I described how she had become a different person from the one I knew. In the new photographs she had gained weight and I could not recognise her. I regretted ever penning that letter. Seeing things through the lens of my prison experience distorted reality, and my perspective was outmoded, antiquated, and not useful for personal relations, I later came to learn.

I talked to older married prisoners about how to handle this bizarre family situation. David Tharazimbi had six children at home in Pimville, and had been sentenced to eighteen years in 1978. His friend, Mzi Khumalo, was philosophical about the whole issue. He probably had a family in a sticky setup too. They said all one could do was accept the reality that your family as you knew it would never be the same again. They told stories of wives who came to Cape Town on gallivanting missions with their secret lovers, using the South African Council of Churches facilities that provided support for the travel and accommodation of prisoners' family members. The couples would be seen strolling in the streets of the city or having fun on the sandy beaches. When these stories reached the prisoner, the poor devil would be consumed by wild imaginings and worry.

The knowledgeable elders in the prison community, the generals as they were called, would walk with you in a 'prison taxi', showing you how helpless you were in these matters, how you should take it, and how your character would be improved by the experience. Either it would strengthen your marriage, or it would destroy it.

Once we had been moved to E Section, near the kitchen and the prison community hall, the morning visits to the dispensary for the collection of medication to treat stressed prisoners seemed to increase and become longer. Standing with that group and listening to their troubles would make you laugh and realise that your own personal troubles were insignificant. They spoke sheer nonsense.

At about this time I also came across Johannes Boyce Bohale in G Section. We had been at school together, and he'd skipped the country in 1976 and trained as a guerrilla, but was captured when he returned to the country. He was subsequently sentenced to eighteen years. At first he didn't recognise me, but about a week later he remembered. A long stay in detention and prison affected one's memory of people. Boyce was known as Zero on the island. In E Section I encountered Gasiitsiwe Mangope, who was serving three years for PAC activities. He arranged that we share the bunk bed in cell 28. Also in the section were Khotso Seatlholo, the leader from the Soweto Students Representative Council who had been arrested in Soweto; and Themba Jack Pikwana – known as Jack-Sue – who had been on trial at the same time as I had. His longing for his beloved Susan was a constant refrain. There was also Mnikeli Williams, who organised a collective of comrades to acquire extra goods from outside. There was Tom Manthata, whose Black Consciousness credentials were being questioned. He claimed to have moved to the United Democratic Front, even though he still advocated the same views that everybody was familiar with. Manthata saw to the welfare of detainees and political prisoners for the South African Council of Churches. He had been convicted for the Sebokeng uprisings in 1984. Dikonelo's father, Leonard Mosala, was with him in detention without trial for a year in 1977 in Modderbee Prison. He was also friendly with Mothobi Mutloatse.

Khotso and Tokyo each separately asked me to be available for the General Recreation Council. Tokyo said it had useful benefits, as the administration experience would be of value in political structures outside prison. Khotso's opinion was that it was important to have all the political parties represented in prison community activities. The PAC was hesitant, but I was nominated onto the executive committee as organiser.

The recreational council used Mallinicks Attorneys to handle their affairs. Judy Moon and Willie Hofmeyr consulted with us and provided sports equipment and entertainment videos. The council had a balance of R63 000 in its coffers. I was told that Jafta Masemola, a stickler for discipline and minute details, had worked out that the interest earned on the prisoners' combined monies from bursaries and other emoluments had accumulated over time in the prison's bank account. After failing to convince the authorities that such monies existed, Masemola launched a solo hunger strike, demanding that the money be made available to the prisoners. He won hands down. The administration removed him to Johannesburg Prison, presumably to place him in unfamiliar territory, where his influence and power could be curbed. He was a strong critic of collaborating with the settler-colonial authorities to get favours or early release.

The 63 grand was monitored by the law firm on behalf of the prisoners. The recreational council supplied equipment for various sports and games, from football, rugby, tennis, cricket, and volleyball to boardgames like morabaraba and chess. There were jazz, reggae and Afro rock music groups too. The annual Summer Games were the year's highlight, in addition to the Grand Finale Arts Festival, which closed the year and was held for a day in the prison community hall.

Each of sections D, E, F and G had football teams. The main rivalry was between the combination of D and F versus E and G. I decided to join the referees' association, and we used the FIFA rules. Barry Pule knew the latest updates to most sporting codes.

There had once been ballroom dancing, but this was scrapped because it made the dancing 'couples' too cosy with each other and led to sodomy. I had heard about this from the older generation, and they said that the fights among prisoners were very vicious at times. That led to retaliatory activities, rather than the character-building political schooling that Robben Island came to be known for.

The ere were few PAC members compared to the influx of convicted MK prisoners in the 1980s. Many Poqo-era prisoners, who had served long terms of up to twenty years, were released at this time. John Ganya and Mgxaji, PAC stalwarts who had served time in the early period and again in the 1970s, knew the history of the prison well. I also spent time with ANC stalwarts such as uBaba Meyiwa, uMfene'ndala and their co-accused in the Harry Gwala case. They had all experienced low and dark moments on the island, and had stories to tell about almost every high-profile person and their idiosyncrasies while in prison.

I soon came to know every prisoner (there were 346) by name and by sight. Khotso was a brilliant student and a wise political analyst. He had completed a Bachelor of Commerce degree in record time and was then in his honours year. He was a critical thinker and told me that if I wanted to have a discussion on the ANC's policies in order to clearly understand their standpoints, particularly regarding the Freedom Charter, it would have to be with Andrew Mapheto. Ranjo, as we all called him, was not yet nineteen when he was arrested for MK activities and sentenced to a long term in prison. His father was a priest at a Baptist church in Mpho Section in Tembisa. He let the Azanian People's Organisation use his church for meetings with community members.

Ranjo invited me to his section to discuss the possible outcomes of the imminent discussion regarding a political settlement that was in the air at the time. He had majored in psychology in his degree. He had a pretty girl's picture on the wall and told me that this was his ideal girlfriend. I couldn't help but laugh. He had a gap in his front teeth like the one-time heavyweight champion boxer, Mike Spinks. Ranjo was concerned that the struggle would have a scorched-earth outcome, and pointed out the need for negotiations at the right time. I told him that the Paris negotiations about Vietnam had occurred while the Vietnamese revolutionaries were still annihilating the belligerent US troops in the battlefield. His point, however, was that the balance of forces between the South African regime and what was known as the Mass Democratic Movement was in the regime's favour.

Political changes and new developments were now happening thick and fast. For instance, in Namibia, independence loomed and was contingent up on the withdrawal of the Cuban troops in Angola. The South West Africa People's Organisation was demanding the implementation of United Nations Resolution 345, while the Pretoria regime was using the communist threat as an excuse not to grant independence to the country. When the Eastern European Warsaw Pact countries started falling like dominoes in 1989, we could see it spelled the end of the Soviet Union. These events brought about animated discussions among the prisoners, particularly those who had received their training in countries such as Erich Honecker's German Democratic Republic. The people marching in the streets in East Berlin, Vienna, Warsaw, Bucharest and other cities had brought down and defeated totalitarian regimes. In China there was the Tiananmen Square incident, and questions about democracy were at the top of our agenda.

By now, Nelson Mandela was engaging the PW Botha regime in secret discussions, yet we knew this was happening. When the National Party's leadership changed hands from the stroke-stricken PW Botha to the left-handed FW de Klerk, the momentum of the talks increased and some of the ANC Robben Island prisoners were called in small teams to the mainland to consult with Mandela. They came back convinced that he was doing the right thing. On one occasion, I heard uMfene'ndala claim that Mandela was selling out. However, he had only asked for brandy and sipped it the whole afternoon while the briefing took place. He came back to the island sauced.

Those were interesting times in prison. I was in a team of writers wanting to collect prison poems. The team comprised Stanley Motimele, Mikki Gxayiya, Martin Sehlapelo, and a few others. Motimele was a member of the African Writers Association. I was also running political education classes for the PAC members in E Section. I referred to how the Pan-African Jomo Kenyatta, while in prison in Kenya, had been tempted with compromises by his oppressors. They had offered him what were effectively golden handcuffs, bonds equally as restrictive as the normal steel ones. At the same time, I registered for degree courses at the University of South Africa. Of course, there was also menial work to be done, and I was tasked with cleaning up the office of the warder in charge of the kitchen.

In the political classes, we had a dissenting voice in a young fellow who crossed the floor from the Black Consciousness organisations to join the PAC. Next, he claimed we were indoctrinating him with Pan-Africanism and crossed the floor again, this time to join the ANC. In fact, he was a rogue soldier from the SA Defence Force who had been convicted in the Free State courts and sent to Robben Island to serve what was rumoured to be four years.

It must be said that the PAC had its internal disagreements. The elder comrades, Ganya and Mgxaji, refused to accept the leadership of Clarence Makwetu when it was announced that the newly launched Pan Africanist Movement (a front organisation for the banned PAC) had elected him as its president. They referred to instances in the past when he had allegedly refused to take up leadership responsibilities in the underground structures and expelled activists from his home. Things were complicated further when they referred to instances in the 1960s when he had driven a wedge between rural and urban politics within the organisation. On the other hand, comrade Zulu endorsed his leadership.

My Marxist piece on labour unions had apparently riled the PAC leaders in B Section. The anti-communist elements even accused me of being a secret member of the disbanded Azanian People's Revolutionary Party, which formed as a result of a split at the abortive 1978 Arusha conference and was led by TM Ntantala, commander of the PAC's armed wing. At the time, he had opposed the leadership of PK Leballo. Blacks Joyi, a PAC cadre who loved sports and physical exercise, spent time with me in the study group that was part of our formal education programmes and in gym sessions, where he played a critical role in training the team. He and I were said to be advancing communist conspiracies against the party.

Prison conditions were onerous and depressing, especially when one's fellow comrades refused to take things at face value. In addition, the authorities had a divide-and-rule approach, which often set one comrade against another.

We codenamed comrade Zulu B-52, to prevent eavesdroppers knowing about whom we were talking. He was an old APLA high command leader, and he clashed over military matters in prison with Jan Shoba.

All prisoners on the island were compelled to sign indemnity forms and non-violence disclosures on entering the prison. These, too, were part of the divide-and-rule strategy. Mgxaji was said to have signed the forms, although he said he had not. The B Section leaders expelled him. We decided that the thinking in this regard was wrong, and stated our position. Before we knew it, a letter of expulsion was sent to Bandile Blacks Joyi, Thozamile Tiyo, Vusimuzi Mandoyi, Mnikeli Williams, Fikile July, Norman Moloi, and me. This was not rational. Nor did it reflect the procedural processes of discipline and political censure in the PAC code of conduct.

We, all the expelled, including John Dlevalile Ganya, did not have problems with the ANC cadres on Robben Island. We were all compatriots and our political differences did not stop us from being friendly. The sulking B Section comrades in our leadership were behaving immaturely. They were also dividing us in the party into conformists and nonconformists. Objectively, the jail conditions had had a deleterious effect on them and adversely affected their actions. Subjectively, we each had to do our best to overcome the concrete walls of the dungeon, which were both physical and metaphysical.

Blacks and Tyson represented the PAC in the Conflict Management Committee, which included the ANC's Jeff Radebe and Naledi Tsiki, and Mzukisi Madlavu and Khotso Seatlholo from the Black Consciousness Movement. This committee also served as the hunger-strike preparatory committee, which facilitated a consultative process that eventually challenged the prison administration over increased violation of the regulations. The warders made life difficult and were intent on breaking down those who defied them.

In May 1989, the ANC proposed, nay stated, that a hunger strike would be started in two days' time. The announcement was made public by the internal structures of the United Democratic Front and from the ANC head office in Lusaka, Zambia. Their political demand was the release of political prisoners, as stated in the Harare Declaration, which had been made by the Frontline States in concert with the liberation movements represented in the Organisation of African Unity's Liberation Committee. The uncles from B Section, B-52 and his friends, decided unilaterally against participating in the hunger strike. The whole of the PAC was compelled to meet and discuss a coherent response to the call for a hunger strike. The 'expelled' group came to the meeting prepared to join the strike, in spite of our objections to the way the ANC had forced its programme onto the community of political prisoners. An overwhelming majority decided that they would join the hunger strike while expressing strong objections to the ANC's authoritative tactics.

The prisoners' team of trained medical personnel, which was made up of Vijay Ramlaakan, Popo Maja and Sibongiseni Dlomo, suggested that sugared water be taken during the hunger strike, and that those older than 52 should be exempted because they would be endangering their health. All the necessary precautions were taken.

The strikers were weighed and had their urine tested every day. The first to fall was the PAC's Magagula. He was taken to hospital on the mainland. Others secretly took to eating. Their names – among them that of Stone Sizani – quickly spread through the prison grapevine. I knew that my friend Ranjo was completely against the hunger strike. He believed it was 'infantile behaviour' and 'vainglorious' to weaken yourself in an attempt to get the enemy to relax prison restrictions. Yes, Ranjo loved his food.

By day ten, the legal representatives of the political groups came to mediate and negotiate with the warring parties – the prisoners and the prison authorities – to end the hunger strike. The PAC legal team was made up of Willie Seriti and Dikgang Moseneke. They dismissed the split in our ranks as not worthy of discussion. They consulted with all of us in one sitting, and the hunger strike was called off on the eleventh day.

The authorities agreed to give us all remissions of three months per year served, for good behaviour. Normally, political prisoners served their sentences in full, without parole or remission. This concession meant that some prisoners were released earlier than they had anticipated. In addition, the food was improved and the conditions with regard to visits were rearranged for the better.

To recover from the strike, we started with fluids and soft breakfast-type meals. My weight remained between 78 and 80 kg while in prison. I was fortunate in that I did not have any serious illness other than sinusitis and the occasional cold.

Once de Klerk became president, the National Party sped up the reforms, and in his historic speech on 2 February 1990, the PAC and other organisations were unbanned. The sceptics were shocked by these developments. For us in the liberation movement it meant, as Paul Langa put it, there was no more time for rhetoric and sweeping statements about 'dark forces' and 'evil forces'. Nelson Mandela was released in spectacular fashion on

11 February. Tokyo, Khotso and I, on behalf of the recreational council, approached the authorities to allow television in E and D Sections permanently, because it was no longer viable to keep political prisoners ignorant of the general news.

Regular readers of the *Cape Times* wrote to the editor, comparing Robben Island to a pleasure island. There was violence unleashed on innocent commuters in the trains by trained personnel with blackened faces. The attacks were skilful. The divide between the United Democratic Front and the Inkatha Freedom Party in Natal increased. De Klerk called this black-on-black violence. He set up a commission of enquiry chaired by the liberal Judge Goldstone to investigate its causes. For political prisoners, their release meant going into a reactionary wave of violence that had nothing to do with the armed struggle.

The ANC leadership sent a delegation from Lusaka to sign the Groote Schuur Minute with the National Party and, in essence, this meant that the ANC was signing off on the end of their armed struggle. This decision split the ANC members on the island in two. A group of about 67 met with MK leader Chris Hani on Robben Island to resolve their grievances. Not long after that, Hani was on the run again, hiding in Transkei and protected by General Bantu Holomisa. The Transkei Military Council had taken power in a bloodless coup in 1988. They unbanned the PAC and the ANC and accommodated activists from both organisations and protected their right to organise. The PAC regional leaders had taken part in the coup, and were strategically placed too. Political activities picked up across the country.

Barney Desai was the first returnee of the exiled community. He organised re-entry papers and landed at the (then) Jan Smuts International Airport on 5 February 1990. He was received by a delegation of the PAC that included Mpuka Radinku of the Azanian Youth Unity, Moseneke and Seriti, who doubled as legal representatives, and national executive council members of the newly formed Pan Africanist Movement.

Throughout all this time, I had received a few visits from my family. Once Dikonelo had completed her management course in Bournemouth and was back in South Africa, she brought our daughter to the island when I was allowed a contact visit. Contact in the sense that we talked to one another through a glass panel. The cruel warders ended our meeting prematurely by dropping a metal shutter that prevented us from seeing and hearing one another. It was as if a guillotine had dropped. During her second visit, two years later, we were able to sit together and talk.

My mother also visited me on the island. Her beaming smile was infectious, making the reunion an occasion of spiritual upliftment for me. The police torture, the solitary confinement, my conscience dictating that I had to make the choice to take a stand and suffer rather than betray the struggle, the agony of standing before a court of injustice, the incarceration and leaving behind a bevy of tearful women, my mother kept from seeing her son – it was all hauntingly painful. Seeing her on Robben Island will always remain a vivid image for me. We hugged and kissed; it was a memorable occasion after a long separation. I grew up adoring her and wanting to please her all the time.

Our neighbours, Bra Mike Morobi and his wife, made a visit. Their son, Philip Morobi, was a journalist with the *New Nation*. They had been nominated by the neighbourhood to represent the elders in the area in giving me support.

Our underground network brought Bigman Moeketsi's mother to visit me. Bigman was now in the APLA camps or in operation in the country. It was a way of letting her know that we activists had a second lease on life and would not go down that easily.

The PAC leadership accepted de Klerk's invitation to talks about talks. It evoked varied responses and caused disputes between some members who were not knowledgeable about the internal workings of the organisation. We were an organisation caught on the back foot and losing the initiative to our opponents. I certainly thought that over-democratising the leadership had its weaknesses too. I also thought the leadership needed to take the initiative and be well ahead of the party rank and file.

The PAC president, Zephania Mothopeng, passed away during this period, and Clarence Makwetu took up the baton. The enabling environment for the release of prisoners was now in place. Tokyo and Khotso were released before me. The recreational council then operated with Bheki Cele and Barry Pule, with the prison community becoming smaller and smaller. The warder at the kitchen, where I cleaned twice a week, asked if I had been arrested for criminal activities. He said he found me a gentle person and certainly not a thief, as the contents of his wallet were intact after he'd forgotten it in the office during my shift. We also talked about his pigeons, which he flew between the Free State and the island. He had taken the prison job as a condition of SA citizenship when Mozambique fell in 1975. I asked him about his family and appealed to his humanity, rather than confronting him about the job he was doing. His concern for me was genuine and touching.

During this time, Bheki Cele discussed with me his plans for when he was released. He was going to take a sea cruise for seven days with his wife, from Cape town to Durban. He was a romantic at heart. I liked it that dreams of the future were with us every day; however, I did not foresee a release for those of us in the PAC any time soon. Cele urged me to have a romantic time with my wife on my release. None of that happened. I can't even recall, now, but I might have been released before him.

Late at night on 25 April 1991, the head of the prison came to our cell and announced a list of prisoners who would be released in two days. My name and that of my co-accused were on the list. It was a complete surprise to find PAC names listed, without any 'minute' having been signed by the PAC. The PAC was sceptical of the negotiations proposed by de Klerk, and it was important to avoid joining a circus of Bantustan leaders and the like. It was possible that a Trojan horse was being manoeuvred into the talks to collapse the African revolution.

The next morning, we found that 43 of us were going to be released on 27 April 1991. Madlavu and Monde Khakaza were also on the list; they were adherents of the Black Consciousness Movement, which had also not signed a deal with the Pretoria regime. I ran my regular six kilometres on the sports fields alone, in preparation for the release and to have my thoughts to myself. I was about to be released back into the bigger prison that was South Africa. There was a mist over the island as I ran, and then the sun broke through as I kept running and running. It was surreal. I ran as if in a dream.

Blacks told me that his father would be waiting for me at the dock. Themba Pikwana was in the PAC group set to be released, and was heading to his village, Magogong, near Hartswater. Khonongwe was going to Mdantsane in East London. Njabulo was faced with returning to the violent Natal townships in Durban. We were received at the dock on the mainland like soldiers who had won a war. Of course, this was far from the situation. At the media conference, I spoke for the PAC, Madlavu for Black Consciousness organisations, and Vincent Diba for the ANC.

My brother Joe bought me a one-way R350 air ticket to Johannesburg and found me a seat on the last flight that Friday. I was homeward bound.

18

Because Codesa

Once home, I hit the ground running. I was received by family members at the airport, and a welcome committee made up of my friend Dan Maponya and the PAC branch chairperson, Mindlo Cebekhulu. Once in Tembisa, I was lifted into the air like a soccer star by a group near our house. I said a few words to the crowd of neighbours, although I had never wanted to be the centre of attention.

Dikonelo was renting a flat in a building in Hillbrow, which was where we spent the weekend. It was strange, waking up without the heavy doors being opened by a warder for the counting process. On Sunday I went for a welcome-home lunch with my family in Tembisa and telephoned a few friends. It was Dimakatso Mofammere's birthday, and she cried happily that I had called on her birthday.

My uncle Jack Monageng was in a coma at Baragwanath Hospital. I was told he had been worried about my release when he suddenly fell ill. I went to see him on Monday and took him flowers in a vase; I'm glad I did, as he died in the early hours of the next morning.

It was time to get back to my life. I applied for an identity document and used the shopping vouchers the prison had given me to buy new clothes at the Eastgate Shopping Mall. Fortunately, Skotaville had kept my job open for me, and they paid my first salary at the end of May 1991 at the same level I'd received four years previously. At first it was okay, but when I realised the cost of rent, groceries, transport, the nanny allowance, I asked for a raise.

Before I knew it, I was organising political activities in the emotionally charged and divided Tembisa. A forum to reconcile the warring parties was arranged at a neutral centre in Kelvin View. I was in a delegation of two PAC members in a discussion with community organisations and political parties. The Inkatha Freedom Party stayed away, despite having agreed to attend the meeting. My fellow PAC delegate, Jabu Mayaba, queried this stay-away by Inkatha, and blamed the ANC for it. I could not understand how an absent political party could bring us to a standstill when our mission was reconciliation. He failed to understand my point that we were representatives of the PAC and had to act in our members' interests.

I told the PAC chairperson, Cebekhulu, with whom I had been in the leadership of the Alex Student League in our high school days, that we needed party-building programmes and political education for our new members. In the PAC, for example, we are taught to argue against our opponents with facts, not let debates devolve into shouting matches. We needed to remain dignified and articulate. We were in the business of winning souls and supporters.

The Convention for a Democratic South Africa multiparty negotiations were on the cards. The ANC was moving ahead with this agenda, while the PAC was focused on increasing the armed struggle and pointing out the limitations of the negotiations, which were not transparent or open. The Organisation of African Unity, through the Frontline States, advocated that the PAC join the ANC at the negotiating table, forming a patriotic united front. A united-front conference was held in December 1991 to launch the OAU-sponsored patriotic front. The PAC leadership in exile felt excluded from the decision-making process, and sent some members of the central committee to participate in the national political programmes. This was after the PAC had stormed out of Codesa meetings that were being held at the World Trade Centre in Kempton Park. The PAC delegates, led by advocate Dikgang Moseneke, said their proposals had been rejected out of hand by the ANC, the government representatives, and a host of Bantustan political parties.

Codesa was a mess, a kaleidoscope of ethnic and racial interests aiming to set up a confederate state called a new South Africa. It sucked in all the political structures that agreed with the idea of changes brought about without 'killing the goose that lays the golden egg'. It also said let bygones be bygones. In simple terms, it meant a change of flag and perhaps a black president, but the rest remained intact.

Elsewhere in the country, a low-intensity war was being waged. The internecine violence had moved to the East Rand townships, centred on Katlehong and Thokoza. This area was a hub for national and international flights at Jan Smuts International Airport, for rail transport, and the main road to Natal and the Orange Free State. It was also the main manufacturing zone for a wide range of industries, from metal to pharmaceuticals and chemicals. The petrochemical, telecommunication, and defence sectors also had a significant presence in the area. It was near this boiling pot that the Codesa talks were being held.

As editorial director at Skotaville, I was involved in producing a collection of essays compiled by returned exile Moeletsi Mbeki, an economics specialist who had worked as a journalist in Harare. We were also busy with a collection of essays by Jonathan Jansen, highlighting the emergence of new thinking from leaders who had been in exile in the US, western Europe and Canada. The book was entitled *Knowledge and Power in South Africa*. In a different sphere, we had commissioned Sekola Sello to write a text for the twenty-first celebration of the phenomenal football club Kaizer Chiefs. Sekola had been my mentor in my early years as a writer. As Skotaville approached its tenth birthday, we needed a commercial success to boost its financial state and free the publishing house from relying on donations.

I had also now joined the PAC leadership, at the request of Sabelo Phama. He reminded me that this mission was incomplete after they had, with the late John Pokela, deployed me in politics in 1985. Sabs laughed at me, poking fun at the years I had wasted in prison instead of sticking to the plan in politics. He saw the funny side of my miseries. Jojo Nqandela, a leader in the Pan Africanist Student Organisation, lobbied for me to get a position in the national executive council of the PAC. In April 1992, I was elected as secretary for political affairs.

Sabs arranged that I attend a reorientation course at the school of the Communist Party of China in the winter of 1992. Maxwell Nemadzivhanani, the national organiser, and ten others were part of the delegation. In Tanzania, Mfanasekhaya Gqobose (Oom Gqobs, as he was known) gave me his set of political books to take home. I chose to go to the party school of ideology instead of taking a scholarship to do advanced executive management studies at Harvard University in the US, as Jonathan Jansen had suggested. At the same time, Dr Motsoko Pheko advocated that I do an intensive human-rights course in Geneva, Switzerland, and this I also chose not to do.

I fell out with Mothobi Mutloatse at Skotaville Publishers. My political involvement had become a matter of contention, and it was said that I would make political decisions favourable to the PAC in my editorial work. This was not true. I actually felt at the time that I had been prejudicial against the PAC when I had set aside plans to publish Barney Desai's biography of the slain Imam Haron and other worthy manuscripts written by PAC leaders. In my absence, Skotaville had published Philip Kgosana's autobiography and Sipho Shabalala's economic policy proposal for the PAC. The reason for the fall out was much deeper than that.

By now I was in the delegation set on having talks about talks with the regime's representatives. The PAC leadership was facing pressure from the likes of Archbishop Desmond Tutu concerning our position of continuing the armed struggle while talking with the Boers. I reminded everyone that Ho Chi Minh had sent a people's delegation to negotiate in Paris while Vietnam was still burning and the battle with the Americans was still hotly contested. Similarly, liberation politicians in Zimbabwe had attended the Lancaster House talks in 1979 while the shooting was still taking place in their country. In South Africa, the securocrats were killing innocent people in the streets every day. APLA played a defensive role, escalating its operations. During the talks, I wrote reports to APLA leaders and PAC structures about the thinking of the Boers. I took notes and kept a word-for-word record. Archbishop Tutu, to us in the PAC, was a version of the ANC in church robes. I told the Reverend Frank Chikane in a discussion with the South African Council of Churches, however, that we would restrain ourselves from having a slanging match in public with the Archbishop of Cape Town, in deference to the Christian community.

Suppressed internal disagreements in the PAC leadership were also being voiced in public. The second deputy president, Dikgang Moseneke, made his exit known by publishing his resignation letter in the media and taking a holiday with his family for a month. I learned later that on his return from a crucial fund-raising trip in Abuja, he had been visited by B-52 and his goons at night at his Atteridgeville home on the hill. The goons had demanded that he hand over the money he had collected. I am told that he cried alone in his room at the humiliation and insult meted out to him in his own house, in front of his family, who had been 'sacrificed' in favour of his PAC duties. He had joined the PAC when he was only fifteen and spent ten years in prison, as well as two five-year terms of house arrest under banning orders. After that humiliation, he left politics.

After Chris Hani was killed, in April 1993, the country was poised for an escalation of the armed struggle. Makwetu was given a platform to speak at Jabulani Amphitheatre in Soweto, at a memorial service for Hani. I had gone with him and Lesaoana Makhanda as part of a PAC delegation to express our outrage at the killing. He spoke seven words in isiXhosa and said that today the true leaders told the truth, just as Sobukwe had spoken near Table Mountain in 1960. The master of ceremonies, Murpheson Morobe, then closed the rally, because he felt the amphitheatre was too small for the crowds. It was a genuine point. At the subsequent rally at FNB Stadium, the PAC was side-lined.

The Special Branch made a synchronised swoop on the PAC national leadership at two o'clock in the morning on 25 May 1993. A police officer Swart, of John Vorster Square, knocked loudly at the door of my Santa Fe apartment in Berea and produced a search warrant, before stating that I was being detained under Section 29 of the Internal Security Act. Swart immediately asked me if I had a gun in the apartment, and I answered in the negative. They searched the flat and found a pistol that I had purchased and licensed in Transkei and kept for my protection. I had asked my wife a few days before to put it in a safe place, and she had promised that she had done that. The police found it hidden in the bathroom.

The previous day I had been in Kempton Park in a select committee meeting of the Multiparty Negotiating Forum on behalf of the PAC. I had left at midday to pick up Tsholofelo at her kindergarten and had then returned to Kempton Park with her until about five in the afternoon, when we went home. I took a pile of documents with me to read in preparation for the next session.

After the police ransacked the flat, I was taken to the PAC head office in Marshall Street, where the search continued. The members of the PAC security unit were all detained too. The search continued until about eight in the morning. I signed a list of items they had taken, including all computer boxes and terminals, documents, the weapons found in the security room, and other materials. The secretary-general of the PAC, Benny Alexander, came in as the police generals were about to finish their search and take us, as detainees, with them. The general in charge told Alexander to shut up when he tried to question the raid.

We were taken to John Vorster Square. The other PAC national leaders who were brought in were Waters Toboti, Maxwell Nemadzivhanani, Enoch Zulu (B-52), Solly Skosana, and other middle-ranking leaders. In charge was Colonel Viljoen. He came to greet me in the reception area on the eighth floor and I accused him of turning Percy Ntsala into a defector through severe torture. He denied this and hurried away. I knew I had got to him.

The police made jokes about the death of Chris Hani and played the fool with us. One asked me to answer a riddle, because he'd heard that I was the most intelligent member of the PAC. He said, 'What was the car that wouldn't die on you in your driveway, unlike Chris Hani?' The police looked at me, waiting for an answer. I was not going to play games like that. I glared back at them. He blurted out the answer: 'A Nissan Sani!' All the policemen laughed loudly at this. I reckoned it was Viljoen's way of getting back at me.

The Security Branch planned to charge the PAC leadership with high treason. They had drawn up charges accusing us of disrupting the negotiation process and destabilising the country. About 70 PAC branch, regional and national leaders were held in custody. Seven were members of the national executive council. I was chief spokesperson, standing in for Barney Desai, the secretary for publicity and information, who had a heart ailment. My public statements endorsed the APLA attacks on the regime's soldiers and police.

On the evening of 25 May, Codesa was in session until late, but I only came to know of this later when, live on SABC television, Cyril Ramaphosa, head of the ANC delegation, demanded my release or the talks would be suspended. I have not asked Ramaphosa whether he was campaigning as a family friend or out of a sense of national duty.

After five days in detention, Solly Skosana (a medical doctor) and I were taken to the Johannesburg Magistrates' Court and charged. I faced an indictment of possession of an unlicensed firearm. The court let us out on our own recognisance. The charge was eventually dismissed.

I arranged for my family to live on a leased smallholding near Zuurbekom in the west of Soweto. We had been blessed with a baby boy, Moreotsile, in October 1992. Three months later, the police raided the place looking for illegal guns. It was nothing but harassment. The night before, I had addressed a panel discussion on the PAC's armed struggle, making the point that 'a good settler was a dead settler', borrowing from the colonial British saying in occupied India. I had said that the sooner the land was returned to its rightful owners the better. I drove back from Rustenburg, where this seminar took place, and where the white participants and journalists had been horrified by my statements. They had failed to appreciate the nuance in my presentation. I was being deliberately provocative. This was why, the next morning, the police came calling. They also wanted to stop me meeting with the minister of police, Hernus Kriel, to discuss APLA and police hostilities. I realised I could easily be liquidated, and no-one would care.

I began dragging my feet with regard to Codesa forums. The PAC leadership insisted that I attend, but I learned from Willie Seriti, the PAC secretary for constitutional affairs, that the National Party representative Roelf Meyer did not want me included in the PAC delegation. I did not care what Roelf Meyer wanted. His utterances were part of a divide-and-rule plan. The chairperson of the forum, Pravin Gordhan, accused the PAC of making a mountain out of a molehill, and said that we were delaying the process of the negotiated settlement. The focus was on elections the following year. A transitional mechanism proposed by the PAC was adopted with modifications, and became the Transitional Executive Council. Paradoxically, the PAC resolved to abstain from it. Makhanda and I were then sent to serve at the culmination of the process in March 1993.

Because of Codesa, most of the activists saw a place for themselves in the new parliament. Careerists reared their heads. I was not going to be a politician in the new dispensation. I needed to do something else.

My calling for writing began, and it caused me sleepless nights. I told my comrades in the national executive council that I would prefer not to go to parliament, since the PAC was awarded only five seats in the National Assembly. Mlambo also gave up his position. Benny was on the Gauteng list and was dropped from the national parliament. I was the fifth, and Patricia de Lille was eighth. One of the candidates for the fifth seat had to come from the Eastern Cape, where the double-ballot system had yielded a seat for the province in the National Assembly. I went my own way.

Epilogue

My story is a parable of a poor mother's son from the family next door to your house, as we say in the township. A story of a person who is sweet and kind but caused a lot of trouble. I was incident prone from early on. I was also naive from the fairy tales, the fiction and drama I read as a young boy, thinking that at the end of the story the triumphant hero walks into the sunset with a sense of satisfaction. Far from it, in reality. After the end of apartheid, in 1994, I did not take any position of responsibility in the leadership of the PAC, and I avoided national conferences where the leadership was elected.

The new political dispensation was not viable for me as an activist. Parliamentary politics were not for me. I thought I would rather carve a niche for myself in the commercial sectors. So I took up a position with a listed company to learn the ropes of corporate business. I simultaneously enrolled in courses with a business school to reinvent myself in the new era, observe the main players, support the PAC in its renewal programme, and follow my own star. Most importantly, I would try to mend my broken family by focusing on my duty as a father and a husband. Little did I know that I would plunge myself into a new site of struggle – the economic-transformation challenges. They were, and are, just as real as the struggle for national liberation.

My first experience of these challenges was when, with my colleague Paris Mashile, a highly trained electronics engineer, we called a meeting with the directors of subsidiary companies to discuss his strategic responsibility for transformation and affirmative action. The white men started the meeting with a dirty joke: they asked if Paris knew what the word 'black' stood for. Puzzled and dismissive, he didn't answer. He didn't have to. He was told that it stood for 'bloody lazy Aids-carrying kaffirs'. With that they all laughed at him. Now Bra Paris had a short fuse. He restrained himself, and once I joined the meeting, his opening remarks were about how inappropriate and improper racist jokes were in a workplace where transformation of the top and middle management was a priority. There was a sour atmosphere in the meeting, as we set targets and identified ways and means to achieve transformation. An hour later the meeting ended and we had our own meeting of darkies, where he told me about their joke. What more can I say?

In 1997 I left the company to start my own business. That's a whole book on its own. It is not politics as we know it. It is life, the human condition, and how the more things change, the more they remain the same.

It is important for leaders in business to write their stories. If the new generation lays benchmarks, it must be because they want things to change. The new South Africa is an anticlimax. It is a haven for the exploiters and oppressors under a majority-based black government. I chose to struggle without expecting any reward, except for the return of our land and restoration of dignity to African people. I wanted a human-rights culture where the shape of your nose, the colour of your skin, your gender, your sexual orientation, your social status, and your poor background counted for nothing.